CONSCIOUS COMMUNITY

The Louis I. Kahn Visiting Assistant Professorship
Yale School of Architecture

Yale School of Architecture
180 York Street
New Haven, CT 06520
www.architecture.yale.edu

Distributed by Actar
355 Lexington Avenue, 8th fl.
New York, NY 10017
www.actar.com

Conscious Community was made possible
through an endowment from the Louis I. Kahn
Visiting Assistant Professorship at the Yale
School of Architecture. It is the twelfth in a series
of publications of the Louis I. Kahn Assistant
Professorship published through the dean's office.

Editors: Nina Rappaport and Stav Dror
Design: Manuel Miranda Practice
Copy Editor: Cathryn Drake

Library of Congress Control Number: 2024938593
ISBN: 978-1-63840-094-3

CONSCIOUS

CHRIS CORNELIUS

RODNEY LEON

ABEER SEIKALY

COMMUNITY

The Louis I. Kahn Visiting Assistant Professorship

Yale School of Architecture

TABLE OF CONTENTS

De-Colonizing Indigenous Housing

National Slavery Memorial in Washington, D.C.

Conscious Skins

PREFACE

The Louis I. Kahn Visiting Assistant Professorship is Yale's second endowed chair to honor Kahn. Established in 2004, the professorship brings to the school younger architects who practice and teach, offering them the opportunity to lead advanced design studios and seminars. The Kahn Visiting Assistant Professorship carries with it the expectation that the work of the visiting professors and their students will be published so that others may benefit from the ideas developed and exchanged in the studios and seminars.

Louis I. Kahn (1901–1974), perhaps the greatest American architect of the post-World War II era, was closely associated with Yale as a teacher and practicing architect. Yale is home to his first important building, the extension to the Art Gallery (1951–53), and his last, the Center for British Art (1969–77). Kahn was fresh to teaching when he came to Yale, in 1947, to begin what would be ten years as chief critic in the architecture school. As a teacher, he worked closely with students and encouraged them to go beyond their initial ideas about architecture, as he himself was trying to go beyond his own ideas. Kahn inspired a generation of architects, leading them to new insights that became the basis of their independent work.

In *Conscious Community*, we see three professors focusing on a shared ethos between marginalized perspectives, bringing them to the forefront of architectural design in academia. The studio projects underscore the potential of architecture not just to create spaces but to craft environments.

This publication was made possible through an endowment from the Louis I. Kahn Visiting Assistant Professorship at the Yale School of Architecture. It is the twelfth in a series published through the dean's office encompassing thirty-six studios listed here by year of publication.

Layered Urbanisms, 2007

Gregg Pasquarelli (SHoP Architects)
Galia Solomonoff (Solomonoff Architecture Studio)
Mario Gooden (Huff + Gooden Architects)

Negotiated Terrains, 2009

Jeanne Gang (Studio Gang)
Sunil Bald (Studio SUMO)
Mark Tsurumaki (LTL Architects)

Turbulence, 2011

Christopher Sharples (SHoP Architects)
William Sharples (SHoP Architects)
Ali Rahim (Contemporary Architecture Practice)

Architecture Inserted, 2012

Eric Bunge (nARCHITECTS)
Mimi Hoang (nARCHITECTS)
Chris Perry (Pneuma Studio)
Liza Fior (MUF Architecture and Art)
Katherine Clarke (MUF Architecture and Art)

Renewing Architectural Typologies, 2013

Makram El Kadi (L.E.FT)
Ziad Jamaleddine (L.E.FT)
Tom Coward (AOC)
Daisy Froud (AOC)
Vincent Lacovara (AOC)
Geoff Shearcroft (AOC)
Hernan Diaz Alonso (Xefirotarch)

Cultural Cues, 2015

Joe Day (Deegan Day Design)
Tom Wiscombe (Tom Wiscombe Architecture)
Adib Cúre (Cúre & Penabad)
Carie Penabad (Cúre & Penabad)

Against the Grain, 2016

Marcelo Spina (Patterns)
Georgina Huljich (Patterns)
Dan Wood (WorkAC)
Lisa Gray (Gray Organschi Architects)
Alan Organschi (Gray Organschi Architects)

Future Real, 2018

Kersten Geers (OFFICE Kersten Geers David Van Severn)
Michael Young (Young & Ayata)
David Erdman (davidclovers)

Mexican Social Housing: Promises Revisited, 2019

Tatiana Bilbao (Tatiana Bilbao Estudio)

Within or Without, 2020

Scott Ruff (RuffWorks Studio)
Florencia Pita (Pita Bloom)
Jackilin Hah Bloom (Pita Bloom)
Omar Gandhi (Omar Gandhi Architect)

Reimagining the Civic, 2022

Stella Betts (LEVENBETTS)
Fernanda Canales (Fernanda Canales)
Luis Callejas & Charlotte Hansson (LCLA)

INTRODUCTION

Conscious Community features three Louis I. Kahn Visiting Assistant Professors. It embodies a profound engagement with the architectural thought of the director of studio: indigenous, Chris Cornelius of the Oneida Nation of Wisconsin, assisted by Aaron Tobey; New York-based architect Rodney Leon, assisted by Doriane Meyer; and Jordanian-Palestinian architect and designer and designer Abeer Seikaly, assisted by Gabrielle Printz. With each studio having its own focus, collectively they represent a disciplinary shift toward responsive architectural discourses focused on the space and program of often voiceless communities.

Chris Cornelius's studio, "Decolonizing Indigenous Housing," explores Indigenous housing paradigms in the face of a looming crisis of shelter in the United States and Canada. Rodney Leon's studio, "National Slavery Memorial," reevaluates the space of collective memory in the context of historical injustices. Abeer Seikaly's studio, "Conscious Skins," takes on an integrative view of traditional weaving crafts and modern design principles. Together they exemplify a commitment to redefining the role of architecture in addressing societal and cultural complexities while redefining the architectural subject.

These projects go beyond their proposed physical constructs; they are manifestations of a conversation about space, identity, and memory.

This conversation challenges architectural norms, advocating for designs that view environmental, historical, and social aspects as interwoven elements of the architectural brief. The projects reflect a shared ethos between marginalized perspectives, bringing them to the forefront of architectural design in academia. They underscore the potential of architecture not just to create spaces but to craft environments.

The editors would like to thank the professors and the students for helping to make this book possible. From Chris Cornelius's studio we would like to thank Alicia Jones, Ruike Liu, Benjamin Thompson, Max Wirsing, Shelby Wright, Sasha Zwiebel, and Joon Yun. From Rodney Leon's studio we would like to thank April Liu, Michelle Qu, Shiqi Li, Jingyuan Qiu, Quincy Ding, Fan Yang, Rosa Congdon, Adam Rostek, Mingxi Li, and Janelle Schmidt. From Abeer Seikaly's studio we would like to thank Adare Brown, Stav Dror, Serge Saab, Elise Limon, Hao Tang, Jun Nam, Morgan Kerber, Sydney Maubert, Smaranda Rusinaru, and Taiga Taba.

Special recognition is due to Cathryn Drake for her guiding and precise editorial work.

We extend our utmost appreciation to Manuel Miranda Practice for the graphic design.

We hope this volume stands as a testament to the transformative power of architecture. It represents a movement consistently engaged with its context, striving for social relevance and impact within architecture's academic realm.

Indigenous, Wiikammi, J. Irwin & Xenia S. Miller Prize Winner, Columbus, Indiana, 2016–17, photograph by Nick Zukauskas

CHRIS CORNELIUS

De-Colonizing Indigenous Housing

INTERVIEW

First published in Yale's *Constructs*

Nina Rappaport
What was your impression of contemporary Indigenous architecture throughout your education, and what inspired you to focus specifically on this work as a young architect?

Chris Cornelius
I was thinking about working to create buildings for my tribe, the Oneida Nation of Wisconsin. I wasn't really thinking about all of the potential of what that actually meant; for example, how to push forward the idea of the intersection of culture and architecture. Between undergrad and graduate school I worked in an office in Milwaukee that was commissioned to do a couple of projects for the Oneida Nation, and they put me on as project designer, so that is when I started thinking about using iconography in a better way. Architecture for Indigenous clients was either some sort of zoomorphic thing where buildings looked like a turtle, bear paw, or thunderbird, or just regular buildings that had iconography applied to them. In graduate school I wanted to examine what it means to create contemporary architecture for Indigenous people, and how I could use my own culture as the lens.

How did you team up with Antoine Predock for the school in Milwaukee, and what was the collaboration like in terms of design approach and development?

That was an interesting process because the school had gone through several other architects. They hired a couple of Indigenous architects and weren't really happy with them, so they organized an invited competition. One of the five firms contacted me to be on their team when I was teaching at University of Virginia, but it wasn't a collaborative process at all, and I was asked only because the client wanted a Native American designer. Predock won the competition instead and asked me to join his team after a really great discussion. We were in different places in our careers; I was three years out of grad school, and he was about to win the AIA Gold Medal. He was impressed with the fact

Chris Cornelius Collaborating Designer w/ Antoine Predock Architect, Indian Community School of Milwaukee, Franklin, Wisconsin, 2003-07, photograph by Tim Hursley

that I was trying to do something different with Indigenous architecture, and working with him on the team was like going back to grad school.

Where do you feel you had the most impact, and how did you integrate Indigenous culture into the project?

I was looking at how things get translated through culture within the school's design. We changed the way we talked about different spaces and institutional labels. We didn't call the place where they eat the "cafeteria," and they still don't call it that; we call it "feast." We don't call the entry space the "lobby"; it's called "community," and the theater is "drum." That is where my voice is most apparent. Each room has a name that resonates with the cultures involved in the project.

How do you even define what is Indigenous architecture, and how is designing from that perspective different in the United States compared to local architecture in Ghana or India? Do these architectural forms respond to a concept of a new postcolonial architecture?

Part of it comes from my own sort of hunch. I start from the existence of such things as Indigenous epistemology and ontology. If we borrow those terms from Western academia, that is where it would end, meaning that colonization wants to compartmentalize and categorize things to discard those that aren't important and give them a hierarchy. I am more interested in the epistemological idea that includes both Indigenous knowledge such as stories and this notion in indigeneity about dreams, visions, and things that aren't provable. Even in grad school I was really compelled by the Oneida creation story. My culture started in the sky on the back of a turtle. It is spatial and full of human and nonhuman characters that have importance. The forms of Indigenous architecture historically came out of cultural understandings of the world, nature, materials, inhabitants, landscapes, and climate. I'm not so interested in replicating it, but rather where these forms come from. How did they arise and how should we be thinking about them in the twenty-first century? I am interested in why certain cultures build tepees and others build wigwams or kivas. Indigenous architecture is a way of thinking as opposed to a style or type; it is really about reciprocities and a way of seeing the world.

Do you think it's the openness and the approach to understanding what is local or the spirit of a place, regardless of a group's heritage? In other words, if you were to design something in another place, wouldn't you find the same spirituality and connectedness, not only because of Indigenous culture but because of your own approach? Is there even a way to describe that? Is your focus oriented more to a spiritual connection than a design?

I understand what you're saying, and it is a very deep question. It goes so deep that it digs into areas that I personally couldn't get to, and here is one example of that. There are Indigenous scholars that say, for instance, that you won't be able to fully understand the idea of Indigenous knowledge without being a native speaker of the language. I don't speak my own language fluently, but there are certain sounds that if you haven't made them by the time you are twelve years old you won't physiologically be able to make them ever. Then there are ways of understanding how you would interpret the language; for me that is a super-deep dive, and it is also connected to the landscape. So yes, I think that, wherever you are in the world, in understanding that connection to the landscape you can only really scratch the surface. You should focus on that first instead of looking at the architecture. To distill it down to material availability and climate are certainly factors, but not the only ones. It is a really challenging question, especially in Indigenous architecture, to know another worldview—were they a mound-building culture, were they nomadic so they had tepees or other sorts of impermanent structures?

So it is more a holistic, spiritual, and anthropological approach to building structures than an artistic or cultural endeavor.

Yes, we don't really separate religion, politics, agriculture, economies, and architecture. No one is having a discussion about architecture; it's just how you live, it's ceremonial. The idea of building things—how you build them and where you get the materials from—is all part of the culture. I can work with other Indigenous nations because I understand not only what to look for but also that I have to learn what it is I'm looking for. I can't just produce the same thing everywhere; I need to have a methodology. Part of that is thinking about the design process as a ceremony. Then how do I teach that to students? We don't talk to students about the value of subjectivity and how you know what you like and why you like it. So if we think of drawing as a ritual, what happens when we start to draw things and we don't know what they are yet? As architects we have to formulate what the thing is; I conceive it in my mind

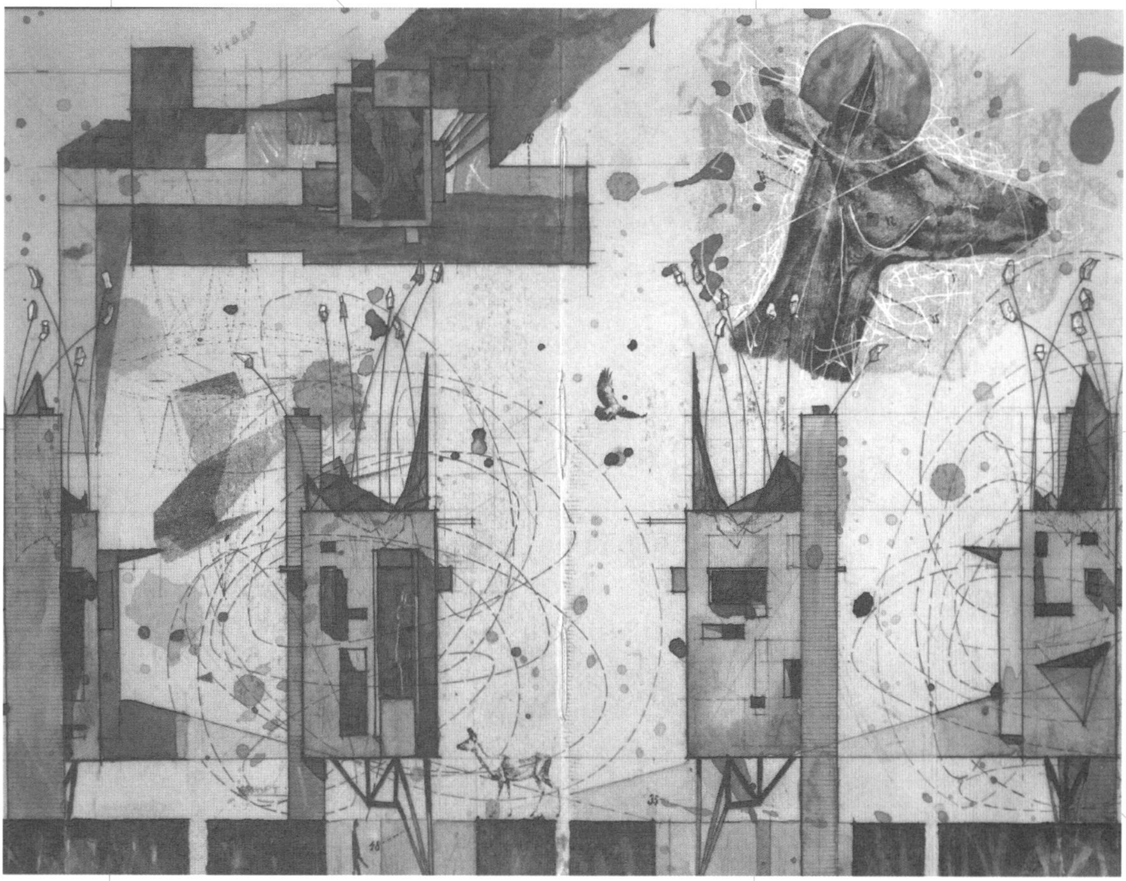

Chris Cornelius, Thunder Moon in the Domicile series, drawing, 2017

and then I can represent it. I always show Robin Evans's "Arrested Image," where he has the designed object in the middle and shows ways of representing it in a triad. What if that was a two-way thing: could representation actually inform the designed object? I teach students how to draw so that it is possible for the representation to affect the designed object in a reciprocal relationship. Dreams are important in Indigenous cultures, along with inducing dreams or putting yourself in situations to promote dreams, like not eating for days. What would happen if architects just allowed themselves to draw without an outcome in mind?

That would be like a ritually induced automatic drawing. Your own drawings are really expressive, lively, and intricate as well as part of a storytelling process separate from representation, along with your models. Do you consider them a project in themselves or storyboards to design a building?

They are all of those things. I started to remove the contingency of what something is going to be. I gave myself an assignment to explore this type of drawing and to think about telling a story when I made physical models—almost like an ad-lib story, where you don't predetermine the narrative arc. I've built a couple of installations that have been loosely based on those models, and now I am looking at what happens when I translate that into a full-scale building. I wonder about the dialogue between all of them because I make them on a computer or it is completely spontaneous.

Has your installation in the Canadian pavilion at the Venice Architecture Biennale that I saw in 2018 impacted a future generation of Indigenous architects? Does the group of architects exhibited there continue in a new network today?

It has grown into a great network of designers across the United States and Canada, and the collateral effects are expanding because the Venice exhibition brought a lot of awareness. It went on to the National History Museum of Canada, in Ottawa, and it continues to give us a reason to be together.

What draws you to teaching, and how do you teach students to be aware of Indigenous architecture wherever they go?

I started as a TA when I was at UVA and enjoyed sharing the knowledge and research that informs my own work. I had great mentors. I was an adjunct at UVA for four years and made the jump to Milwaukee for a tenure-track position. My work is about representation: I teach studios in African-American and Latinx neighborhoods, and about hip-hop as a culture. I am interested in how we represent culture as a big, hard-to-encapsulate thing.

Indigenous, Trickster, Sheboygan, Wisconsin, artist residency at Bookworm Gardens, 2018, photograph by Thomas Harris

What are you teaching at Yale this semester?

This is the first time I will do a deep dive into Indigenous content in an academic studio. We are examining Indigenous housing in the Opaskwayak Cree Nation, in Manitoba that I've been working with for a couple of years now. I was brought into the project through a colleague at Minnesota and a community member from the University of Saskatchewan. Their housing is almost the same as my reservation's housing, even though it's a completely different landscape. We will dismantle policies as a way to decolonize the system of building standards based on cultures, labor, and materials. The students will investigate how this notion about Indigenous knowledge—has a specific resonance with us as a culture and in the profession—in terms of how we could think differently about architecture.

STUDIO BRIEF

Decolonizing Rights

The studio “Decolonizing Indigenous Housing” examined one of the fundamental crises facing Indigenous people. Housing is a human right that has been ignored over time for Indigenous people in both the United States and Canada. Public housing has never really served Indigenous people the way it should. In other words, it is a system that needs to be decolonized and dismantled and then reconstructed. The current means by which housing is administered to Indigenous people is fraught with counterproductive bureaucracy and policy. Funding, while not currently sufficient, isn’t the primary problem. It is the very system in which housing is deployed that is the problem. Residential building codes, for example, represent a form of colonization by treating people and structures in a homogeneous way.

This studio started from the principle that building one’s own home is a treaty right in Canada. Indigenous land is sovereign land, and that sovereignty should be reflected in all things, including housing. From this assumption we asked, What if Indigenous people could write their own building codes guided by culture as well as their relationship with the land and all of its inhabitants instead of legal obligations? To support this inquiry, the students worked to identify all of the factors that complicate Indigenous housing. Two factors in particular were set out as being of paramount importance.

The Land

The studio worked with the Opaskwayak Cree Nation (OCN), located in Manitoba, 626 kilometers northwest of Winnipeg, or six-and-a-half hours by car. Separating the city of The Pas from the reserve land of the Cree nation, the Saskatchewan River has always played an important role in tribal culture.

Extraction

In 1876 the Opaskwayak people signed Treaty 5 with the federal government of Canada, giving the tribe timber rights to provide the resources to build their own homes. One of the most visible scars of colonialism is extraction, and forestry in Canada is the embodiment of extraction. Deforestation in the country now exceeds that of the Amazon. This extraction is systemic racism since it supersedes the Indigenous connection to the land and abrogates the official treaties. As stewards of the land, Indigenous people see themselves having a relational connection to the territory. That is to say, the earth is our mother, and we cherish the gifts she provides us. And they are gifts, not commodities.

Methodology

To identify additional factors, along with their complex interrelationships, the students began with a three-week mapping and research phase to familiarize themselves with the OCN. During this phase they examined potential ways to decolonize the map of tribal territory. They looked at how members of the nation have begun to remap their community using the Cree language, demonstrating the importance of the land-language connection. From these efforts the students worked out means of mapping that were inclusive rather than exclusive exercises as they gathered information and reflected critically on how they could visualize their findings, as well as to whom the graphic translations of the physical landscape, cultural terrain, and spiritual setting should be addressed.

After this initial mapping phase, the studio performed a kind of "triage" in which the students identified the problems that need to be addressed. Each student chose areas of concern to focus on for the remainder of the semester. The following weeks constituted the synthesis phase of the studio, with each student taking what was learned from the preceding weeks, reading about Indigenous lifeways, and conversing with members of the OCN to develop a project thesis. Preliminary findings from this phase were shared with members of the OCN community and developed through virtual meetings with Indigenous activists and scholars who shared their insights.

Within this overall structure students were asked to develop their own areas of focus and methods of making to promote as thorough and nuanced an examination of the tribal housing issue as possible. This meant looking at everything from policy to culturally specific technical design solutions in the effort to answer the following questions: What should housing for the Opaskwayak Cree Nation look like? How would it differ from housing for other Indigenous nations? Could we offer similar solutions for other nations in the United States and Canada?

STUDENT WORK

Alicia Jones

Ruike Liu

Benjamin Thompson

Max Wirsing

Shelby Wright

Sasha Zwiebel

Joon Yun

Alicia Jones

Unmapping

This project challenges the dominant Western discourse on housing and architecture by examining alternative ways of conceptualizing and generating space. It is based on the recognition that the very classification of "housing project" is laden with a highly restrictive set of assumptions and values—specifically the Western view of housing as a commodity to be produced, traded, consumed, and replicated rather than as a site with intrinsic social, cultural, and environmental dimensions that impact the lives of its inhabitants.

Addressing these discrepancies, the project draws on Indigenous storytelling as a source of inspiration and knowledge while viewing architecture not as a static object but as a living entity shaped by the complex interplay of people, creatures, and things that constitute the built environment. Conceptualizing the house as a living creature recognizes its agency in shaping human experience while highlighting the importance of a reciprocal relationship between humans and their built environment.

The project challenges the traditional notion of mapping, instead aiming to "unmap" the prescriptive way of thinking about architectural design. It is realized through a series of short stories exploring how a house comes to be and interweaving various scenarios to rebuild a neighborhood of track homes in The Pas. Through storytelling, a new community embodying its own spirit and character emerges. Finally, rather than serving as a new baseline, the project proposes a platform for dialogue and discourse on an architecture imbued with life.

Two views depict perspectives of the Bird Sanctuary Tower: one shows a bird approaching it; the other depicts a wolf hoping to catch the bird before it can enter the structure to safety.

The Fur House is equal parts animal and fungus. This series of frames depicts the process by which the Fur House claims a new host, releasing its spore on an unsuspecting tract home.

The Seasonal Structure adapts to the changing seasons by shedding its shingles in the summer and regrowing them in the winter. This image depicts the structure in summer and winter.

The Tower is built to see beyond the trees and designed to grow taller as the trees mature.

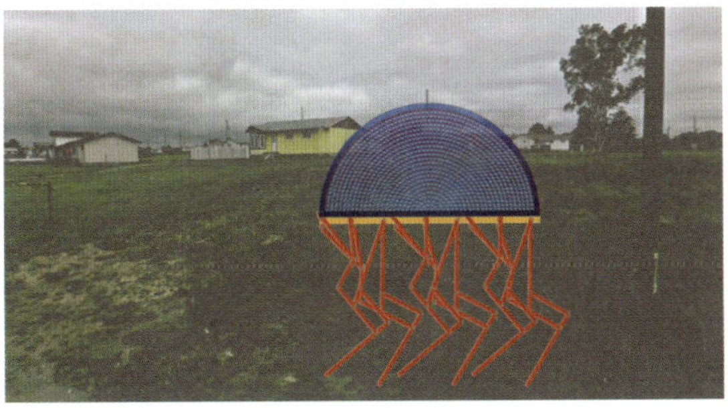

The Pollinator travels through the community, transporting bees that play a crucial role in pollinating plants and crops.

Close-up view of The Pollinator

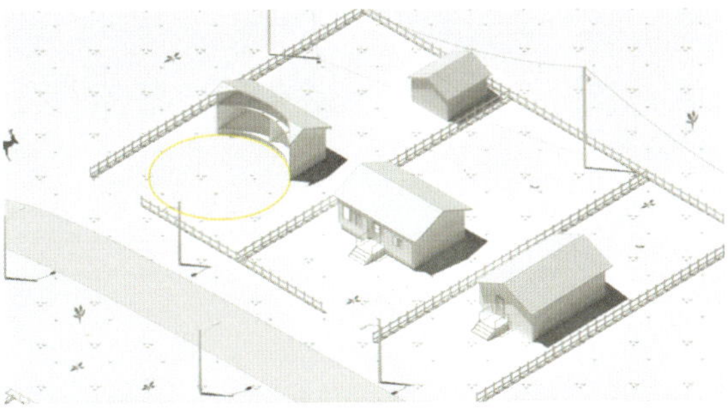

An old tract home is deconstructed to make way for a new greenhouse.

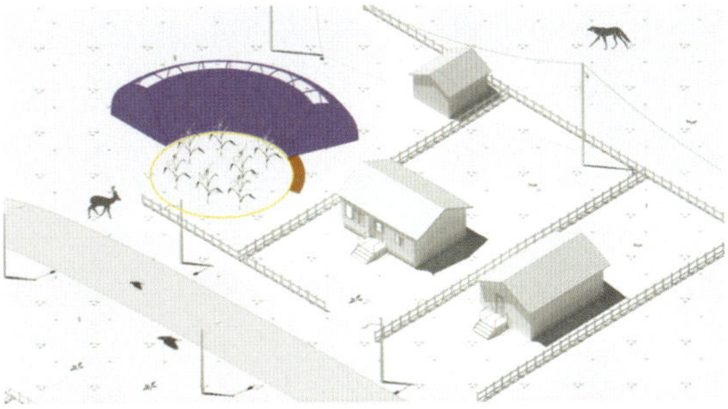

A new greenhouse and garden are constructed to better support inhabitants of the community.

A map meant to obscure information rather than reveal it—an exercise in "unmapping" from the early stages of the project

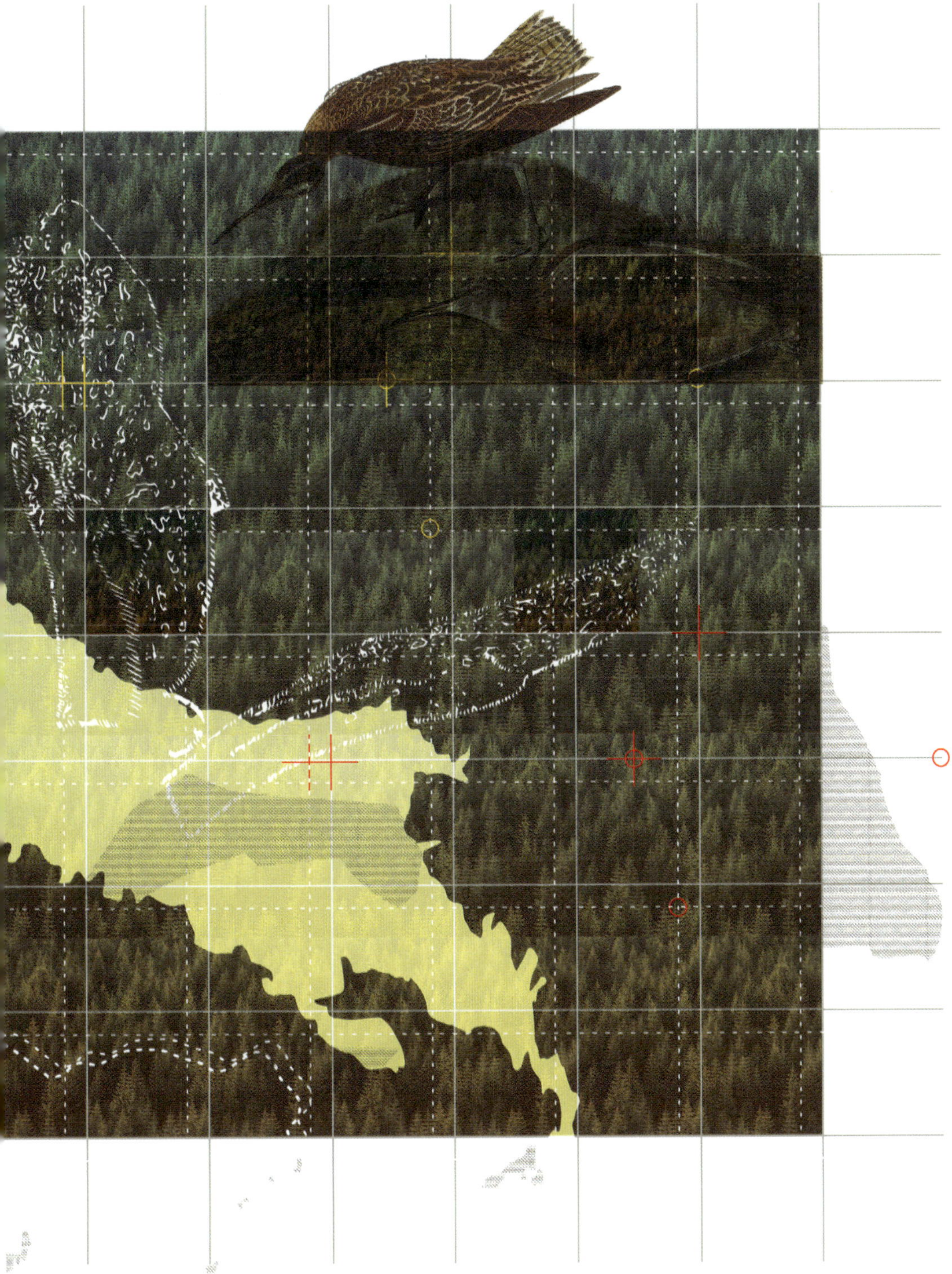

Ruike Liu

Learning from Skateboarding

“Skaters exploit the ambiguity of the ownership and function of public and semipublic space, displaying their actions to the public at large… They bring time, space, and social beings together by confronting the architectural surface with the body and board; as a result, they redefine the city and its architecture, their own social identity and bodies.”

—Iain Borden, “Skateboarding and the Performative Critique of Architecture”

The artistic expression, bodily movements, and rebellious spirit of skateboard culture makes it popular among Indigenous groups as a medium through which Indigenous culture can be brought to public awareness. Beginning with a study of skateboarding on reservation land, the project reveals the skate park as a neutral surface capable of decolonizing the existing context while being indigenized by the First Nation.

My proposal extends the surface of the skate park while creating an indigenized landscape that accommodates the everyday rituals of the local people. The landscape is not still; it follows people’s movements and merges with housing patterns, leaving spaces defined not by rules but by customs and rituals.

Mapping of documentation of the site and Indigenous culture

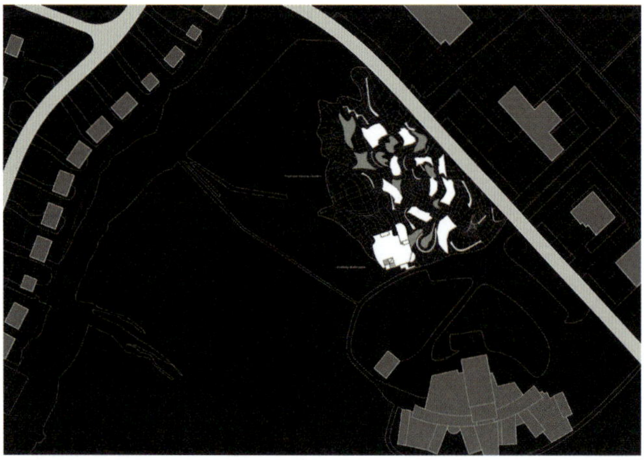

Site plan of the non-grid land

Conceptual site plan of the freedom of the land, houses, and people

From left to right: wandering, walking, sitting; skating, sitting on rooftop; gardening, private backyard

From left to right: drying fish, private courtyard; sitting on rooftop; gathering, sitting, playing, shading

From left to right: gathering, sitting; skating, dancing; skating, walking; gathering, playing

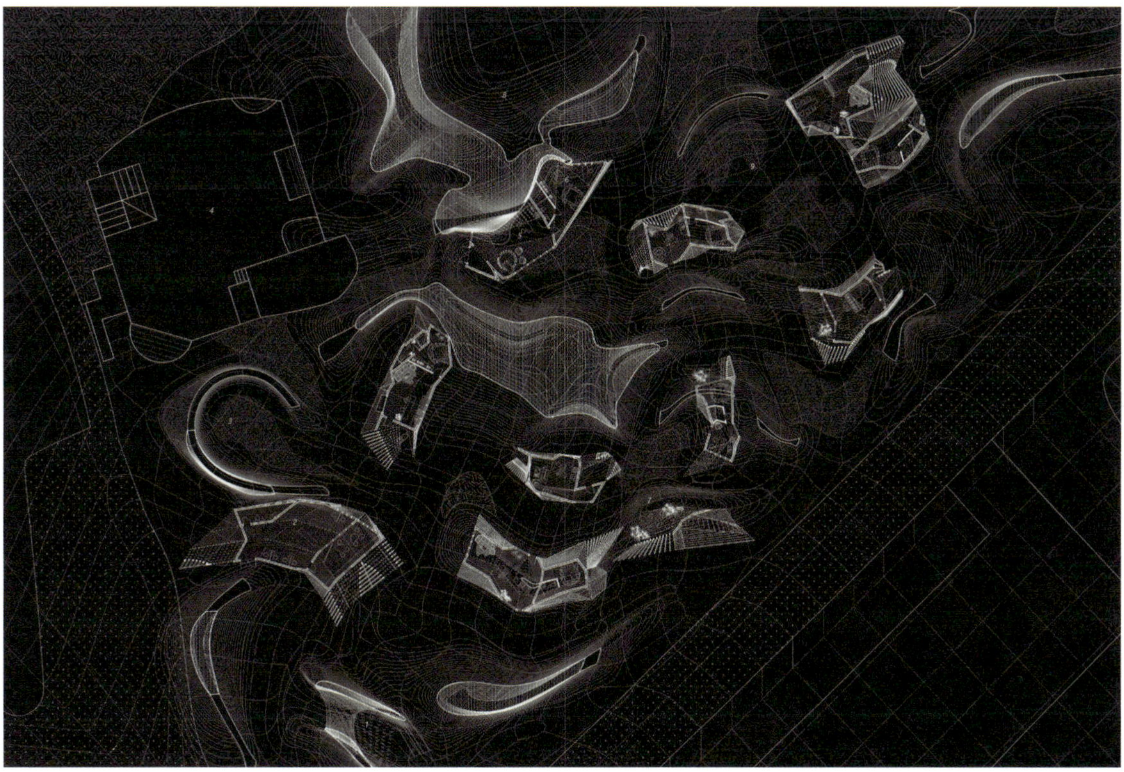

Ground-floor plan showing movement

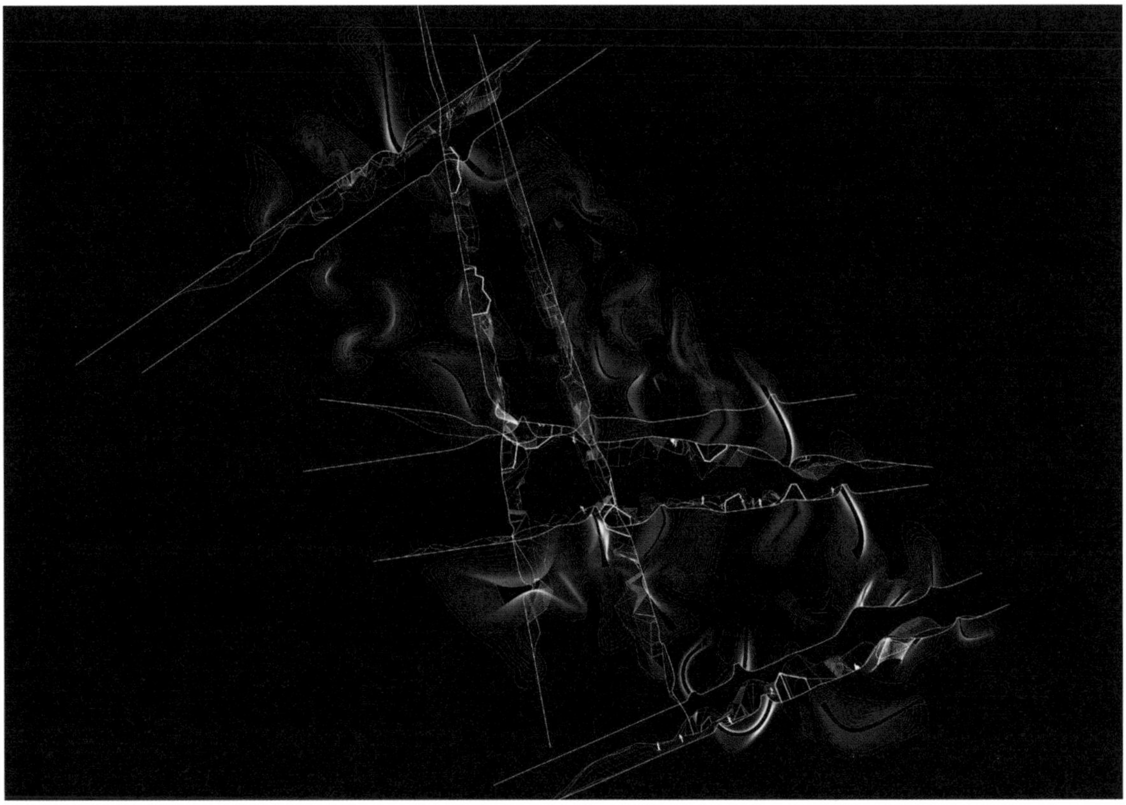

Section showing movement

Aerial view of the land and activities

Interior of a living room that communicates with nature

Exterior showing a path for all speeds

Exterior showing a path for all speeds

Benjamin Thompson

Flock

The houses on the Opaskwayak Cree Nation (OCN) reservation are single-story rectangular structures set along typical suburban streets. Not limited to the OCN, this typology is a lasting, pervasive legacy of colonialism in reservations across Canada and the United States, regardless of culture or climate. This colonial housing typology has made an antagonist of the climate, working against Indigenous people's connection to the land. The project seeks to reinstate that connection and build in a way that is amenable to the region and the Swampy Cree people.

The first set of operations reconnects the house to the earth. This burrowing action has thermal advantages and cultural resonance with the Swampy Cree since the placenta of newborns is ritually buried on family land. This accompanies a strategy of creating soil berms to add a buffer mass, supplementing the construction of rammed-earth exterior walls, extending and strengthening the roof to handle heavier snow loads, and using the snow as an insulator. These spaces have a gradient of conditioning that extends into a flexible space and a completely passive space. This follows Swampy Cree settlement patterns, which consisted of living out of several cabins stretched along the paths of migrating caribou or geese; rather than moving from cabin to cabin, a version of this journey would take place seasonally within the home.

The idea of the "flock" determined how these homes would form a community. Each home is constructed as close to the center as possible and given enough space for additions. The community forms as friends and family build near one another. Roads and footpaths are secondary, weaving through the dense forest where the flock exists.

Hand drawing comprised of several translucent layers produced as part of the studio mapping exercise

Study model of the “flock” created by the aggregation of homes

Site plan showing the integration of housing within the current fabric of the OCN

Subtractive study model fabricated as if carved from a single block of wood

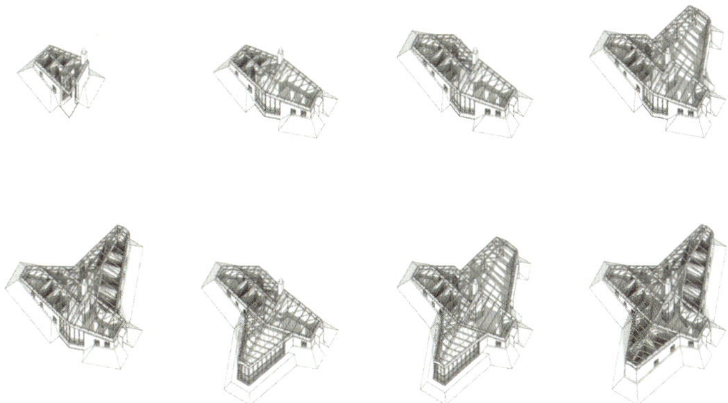

Axonometric drawings of the various typologies of housing

Physical model of the rammed-earth hearth that all housing would be built around

Section perspective of a home under construction

View of the flock of homes from eye level

Interior of a home with animal hides being tanned

Interior rendering of a home with an elder speaking to children

Max Wirsing

Wisakedjak's Bear

The Opaskwayak Cree Nation, located in and around The Pas, Manitoba, is in need of some 880 housing units. The OCN reservation land has been split, fractured, and drawn with lines and boundaries, separating land and people through colonial conceptions of property ownership.

The project builds on a study of Indigenous epistemologies and ontologies, taking inspiration from the poetics of Swampy Cree cosmology and Trickster narratives to decolonize housing for the OCN. Within a framework of storytelling as a tool of form generation and decolonization, Wisakedjak's Bear creates a unified housing scheme across colonial boundaries, stitching together the fragmented parcels of the reservation.

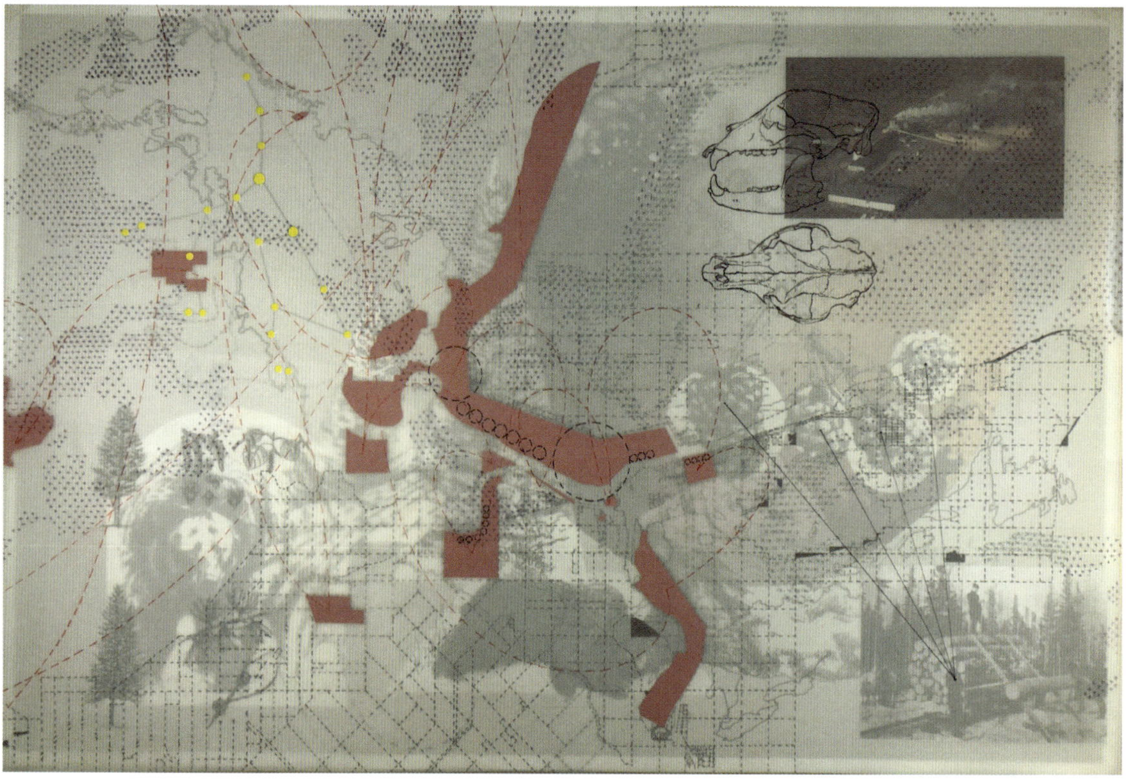

Mapping exercise of the project site, in The Pas, Manitoba, with reservation parcels designated to the Opaskwayak Cree Nation in red

Illustrated interpretation of a Swampy Cree Trickster story. The tamarack trees restrain the Trickster from his own greed so that everyone has a share of the feast.

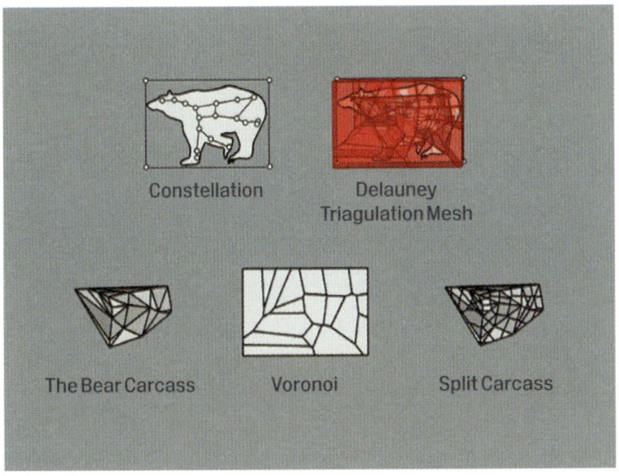

The use of a Delaunay Triangulation mesh creates three-dimensional form out of a celestial constellation, and a 3D Voronoi diagram splits it into discrete masses (housing units).

The facets of individual units key into one another so that the full massing (the "bear") might be unified.

Constellation of the bear mapped over The Pas

Discrete housing units dispersed onto separate parcels of the OCN reservation

Massing models demonstrate how the units fit into one another.

Corresponding dormers and vestibules allow the faces created by the Voronoi to key into each other.

Rendering of project masses

Rendering of one of the project masses

A connection is established to unify the residences as a system and community, despite the fractured nature of the OCN reservation parcels.

Rendering of one of the project masses

Shelby Wright

Footprint Tree

Storytelling is an essential component of passing down generational knowledge in Indigenous cultures. Unlike Western fairy tales, where the moral of a story is clearly spelled out, Indigenous stories take a less straightforward narrative approach, allowing meaningful ideas to be conveyed in an unassertive way.

The project storyboard shows the interconnectedness of humans and their environment. Architecture presents not as a form imposed on a community but as another character in the story. Vignettes are framed in and around architectural moments, which interact with the characters in specific ways. The story ties elements of building into the local ecology and culture. Woven into the visual stories is a retelling of the traditional Swampy Cree tale of the footprint tree, implicating the narrator of the story, presumably a human, as a character whose footprints are no different than those of the animals to emphasize interconnectedness.

From the mud and snow I'd walked in
Sniffing around my feet too.

If the bear was the same one
Who left them behind
Long ago
They would leap back on
The bear's feet
And go back to living there.
Until the bear walked in snow
or mud again.
Those leaves leaped down!
Bear footprints

Made a loud sound
When they hit the
ground
And often
Bird footprints flew
away in the wind
Trying to catch up with
the birds!
Bird-footprint leaves

One time I wished up
a footprint tree.
It had the
footprints
of many
animals
For leaves.
Footprints left
behind
In mud and snow
Were all
hanging on
that tree!
I wished all
kinds of weather
Into that tree, too.
It stayed cold
Around the snow
footprints
And warmer around
the mud footprints.
I wanted them to
stay just as

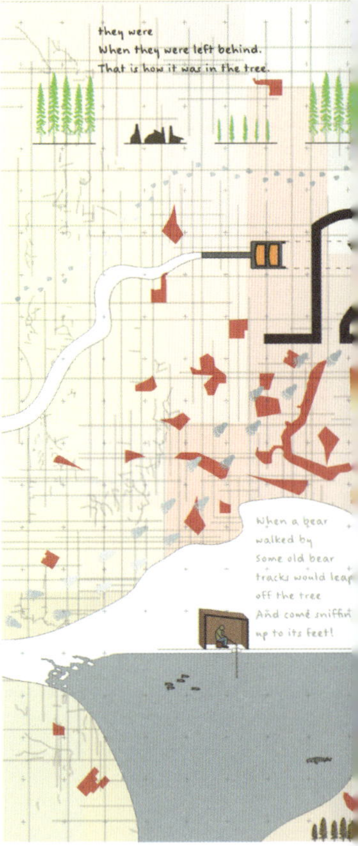
they were
When they were left behind.
That is how it was in the tree.
When a bear
walked by
Some old bear
tracks would leap
off the tree
And come sniffin
up to its feet!

could be seen floating
in the air!
I tell you I was happy after
wishing that tree up!
Except later, I had leaves

From the mud and snow I'd walked in
Sniffing around my feet too.

They would be looking
For a home.

Sasha Zwiebel

Decolonizing The Line: Land, Building, and Representation

To approach the housing crisis for the OCN, this project focuses on the theme of decolonizing the line applied to political borders, land, building, and representation. Woodlands-style painters such as Benjamin Chee Chee (Ojibwa) have used lines to reveal a way of knowing that holds a sensibility of the land and allows for uncertainty, interpretation, and relationality. By learning this and other Indigenous ontologies, I worked to break from the colonial mindset that has fueled the systematic disenfranchisement of Indigenous peoples.

This project proposes a land-reclamation strategy that expands the OCN reserve borders to existing natural edges. This line could be a wholly different type of border as a place to gather, live, and steward where housing aggregates to create communities that protect family hunting trap lines and critical animal habitats, harvest wild berry patches, and watch over the old-growth forest. No line is ever neutral, and thus the power to draw a line must be wielded with care, beauty, and culture.

Combining facts, intuition, and ideas to consider relationality, the mapping included the soils, trees, animals, and reserve boundaries in the boreal forest around the OCN land.

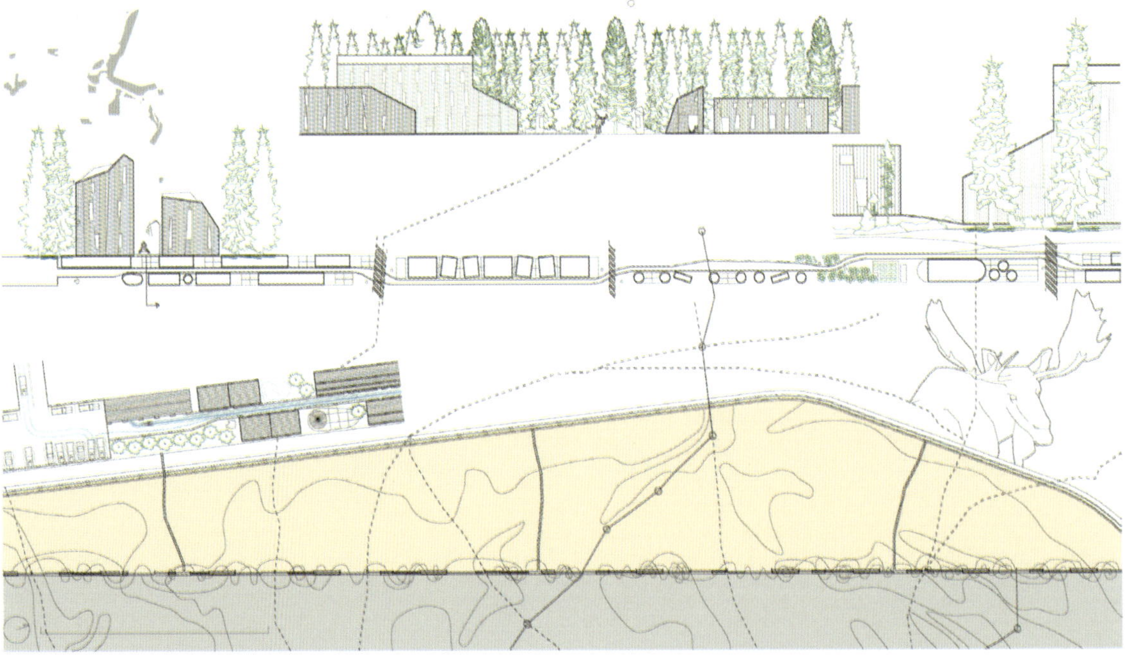

Synthesis drawing at midterm

Final site plan focusing on blending Indigenous ontology with an architectural orthogonal plan

Final model showing the two housing types placed on the natural edges of the boreal forest

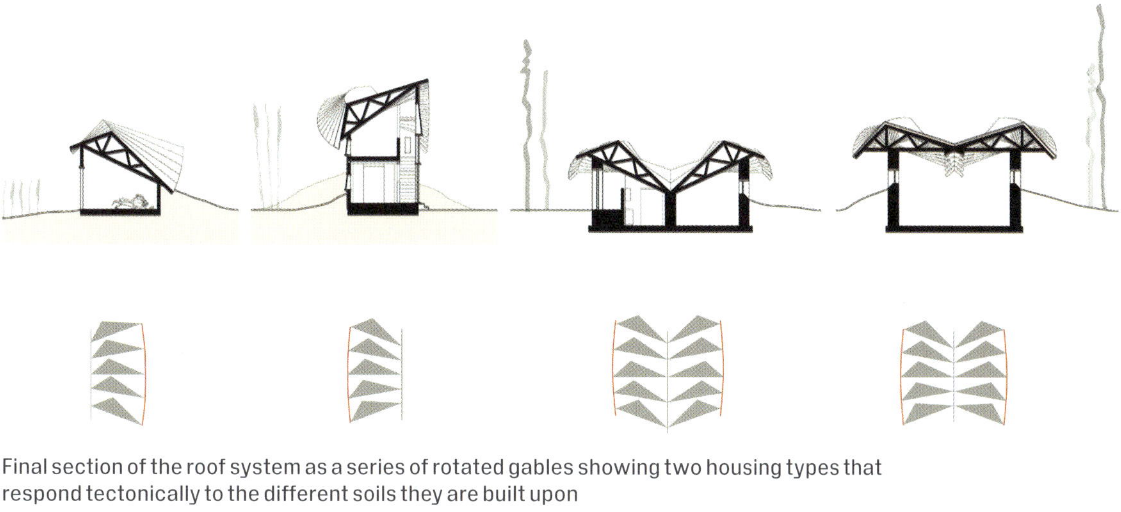

Final section of the roof system as a series of rotated gables showing two housing types that respond tectonically to the different soils they are built upon

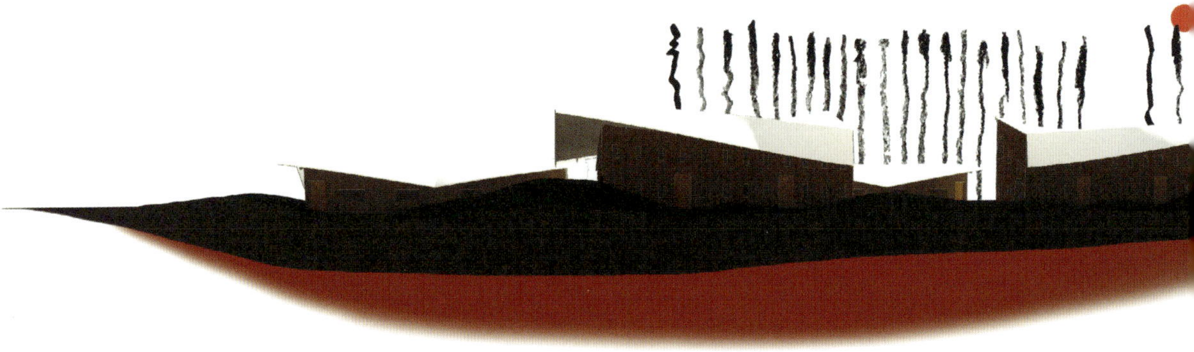

View from a distance

Final model photo

Sketch model highlighting the relationship of home, earth, and sun via manipulation of shadows

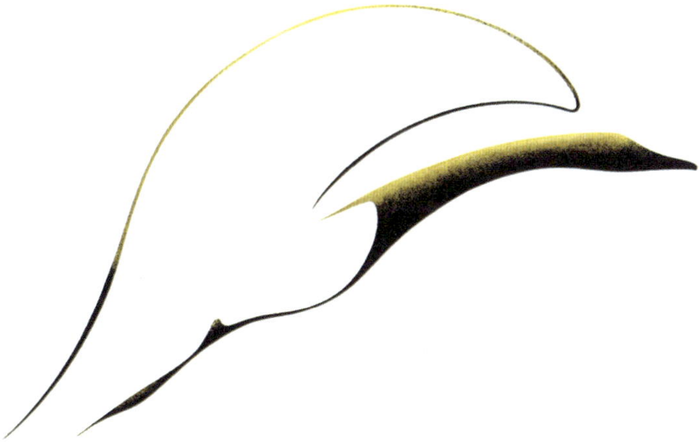

Reference image: *Sun Bird*, by Benjamin Chee Chee

Joon Yun

Animal Perspective

This project explores the concept of the Indigenous world through the lens of Shawn Wilson's perspective on multiple interconnected relationships. Within this framework the research employs a game engine to create a map that includes intangible data such as gravity, time, and locomotion, offering a nonhuman viewpoint of the world. The study examines the site from the perspectives of four animals—deer, muskrat, bird, and wolf—to understand their life patterns and interactions with human infrastructure. Through virtual reality (VR) technology devastated industrial sites are reterritorialized, allowing for a comprehensive understanding of the site from various subjective experiences.

The research focuses on issues of colonization and human monopolization of improved water access, particularly through ongoing hydroelectric projects that have had a negative impact on habitats and water quality. The primary goal of the project is to decolonize the water by transforming the industrial site into a coexisting ground for multiplicity. The design proposal features a circle of multiple ponds that create a diverse ecosystem and facilitate a creative shrinking-and-growing method for decolonizing water.

A transformative house is proposed to adapt to seasonal changes, providing a space for multiple animals to coexist on the same ground. VR and AR technology are used to virtually project digital graphics onto the physical site, challenging existing frameworks and presenting various forms, scales, and perspectives of the space. The emphasis is on the importance of considering the connective relationship between objects in a similar way to the Indigenous worldview, where every object is seen as living.

This research advocates for a transformative and ever-changing typology in human infrastructure to support sustainable Indigenous futurism. By adopting elastic narration and tactical adjustments, human infrastructure can coexist harmoniously with the environment, facilitating a better understanding of the Indigenous world and promoting a more inclusive and ecologically conscious future.

The White-Tailed Deer's Perspective: interaction and conflicts between people and deer

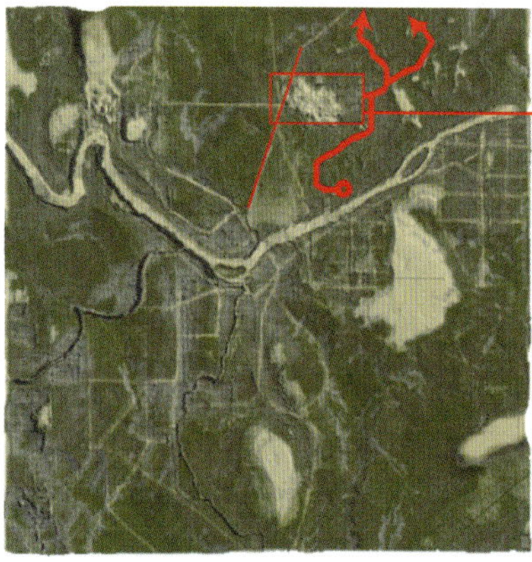

Mapping in unity

Paper mill—
Canadian paper industries

Provincial road—
risk of the roadkill area

Nature—
infographic

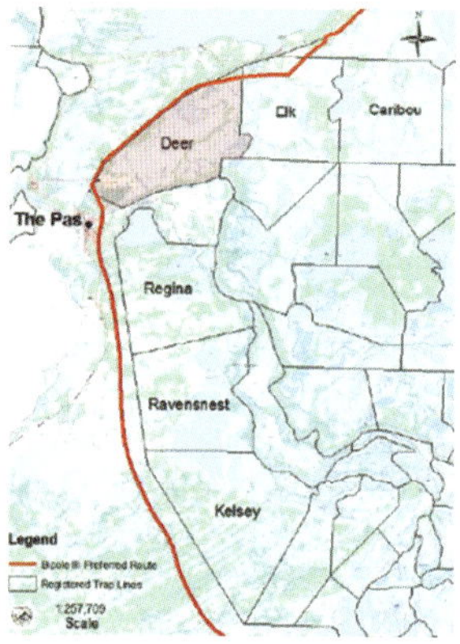

Trap line area

Game-engine simulation

Reterritorialized deer's ground

The Wolf's Perspective: predator and prey relationship, population change, migration

Mapping in unity

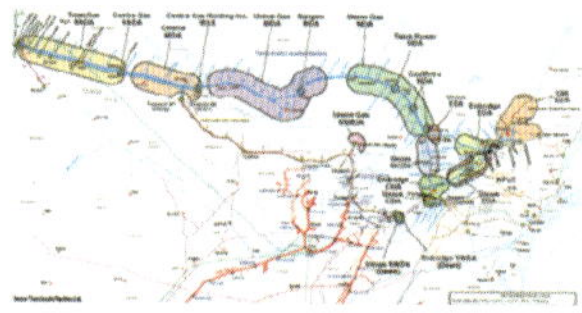

Manitoba dam construction

Wolf in flood zone

Flood zone Nopiming provincial park

Moose carcass

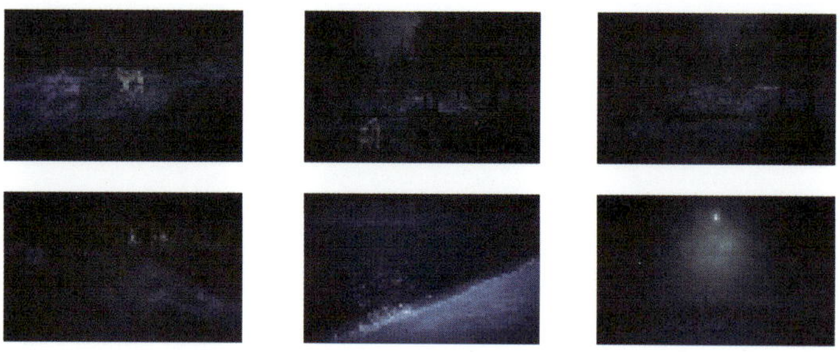

Game-engine simulation

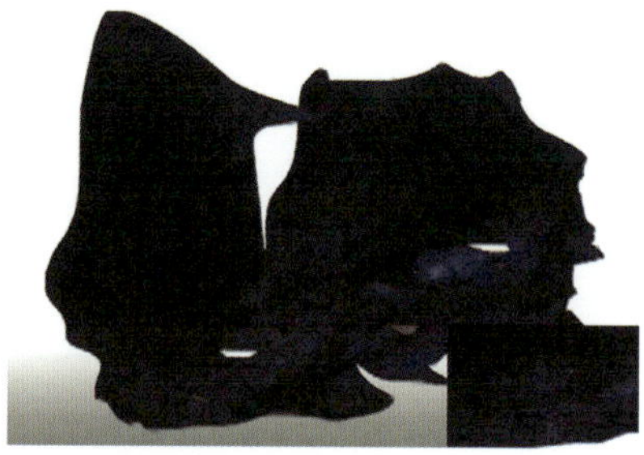

Reterritorialized wolf's ground

The Muskrat's Perspective:
interactive life-pattern base with both geological and biological data

Mapping in unity

Manitoba fish

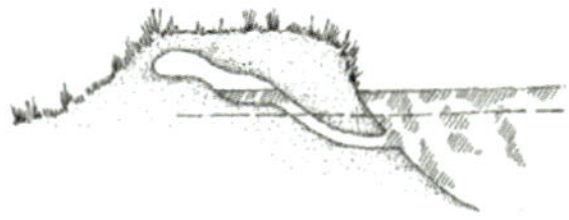

Muskrat dam—flood level

Wetland from Saskachen River

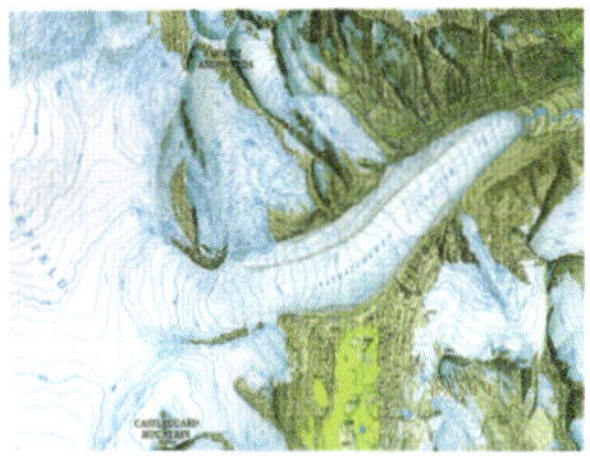

Saskachen River glacier pattern

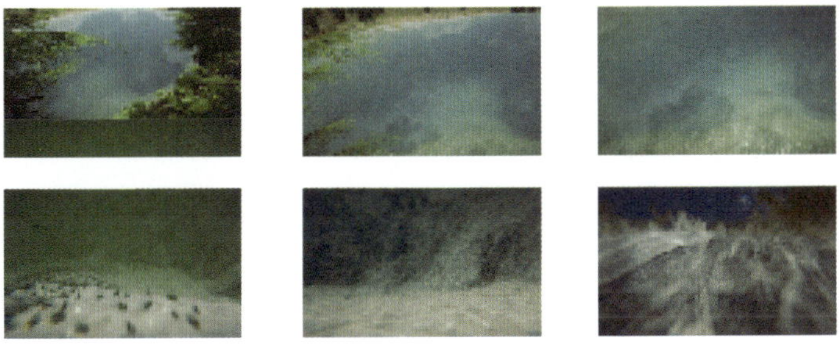

Game-engine simulation

Reterritorialized muskrat's ground

The Bird's Perspective:
interactive life-pattern base with both geological and biological data

Mapping in unity

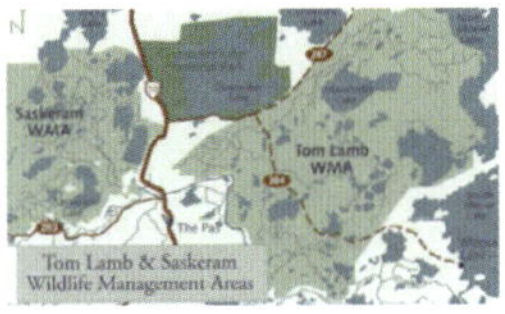

Staging and nesting area

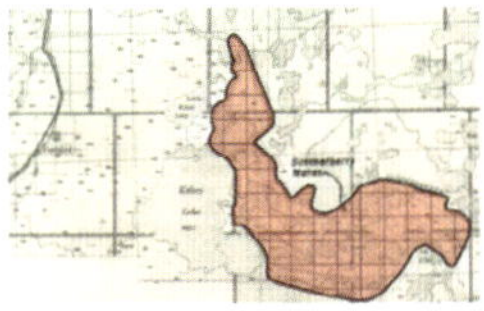

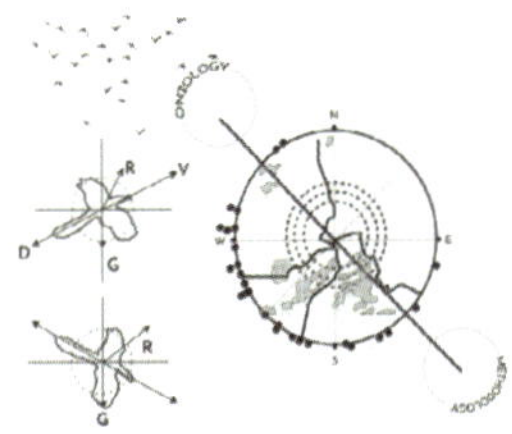

Summerberry marsh and directionality

Game-engine simulation

Reterritorialized bird's ground

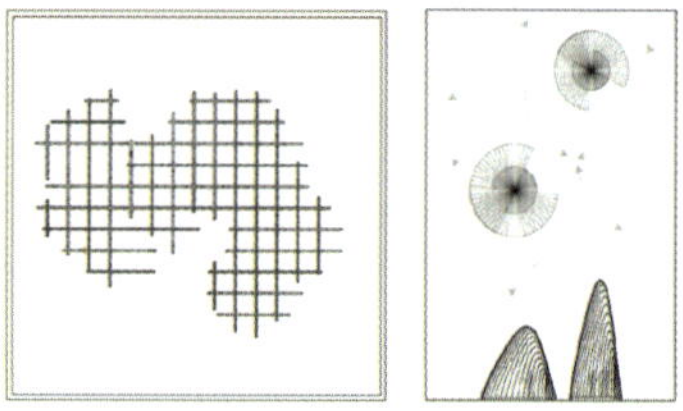

Phase 1: Temporary tipi structure, summer season

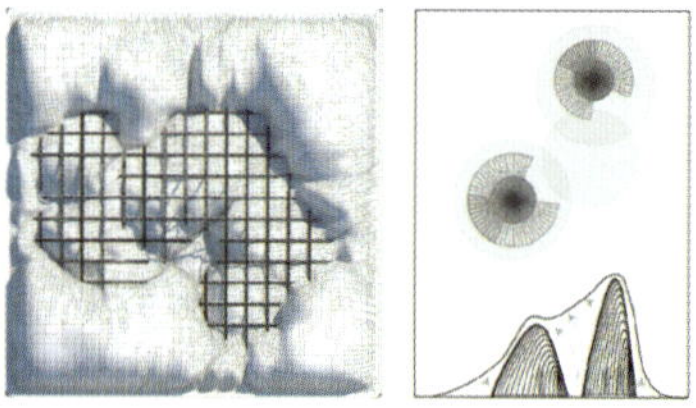

Phase 2: Injecting gas to the void, fall season

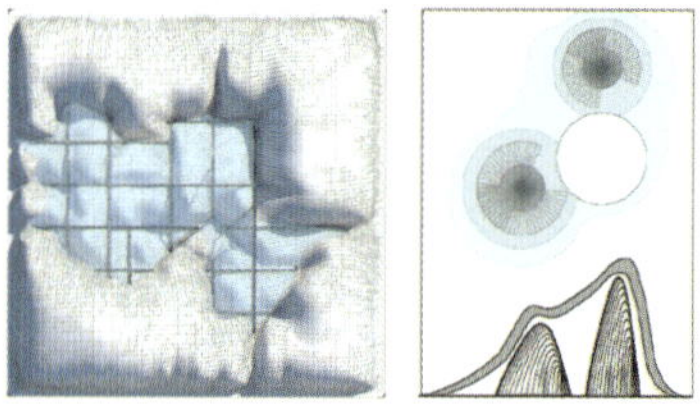

Phase 3: Semi-temporary ice dome, winter season

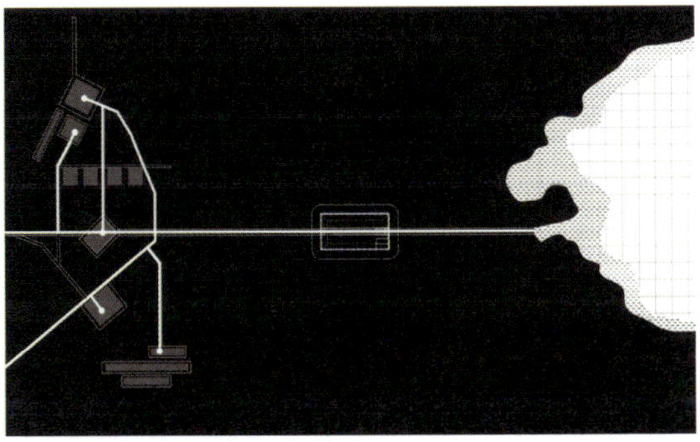

Current Sewage Program

Design Gesture

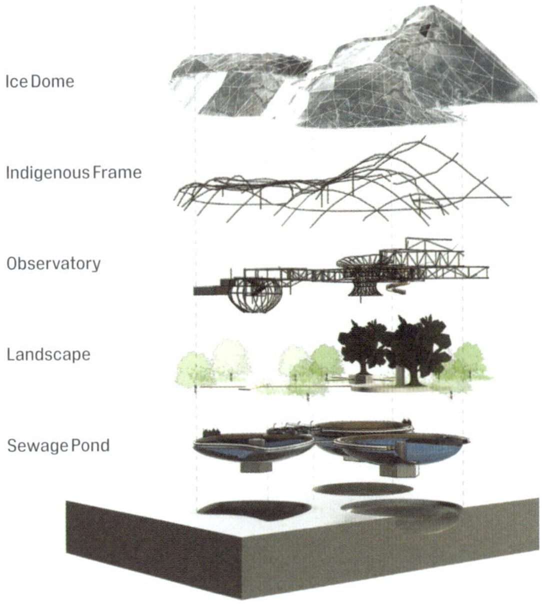

Rodney Leon, Ark of Return, detail New York, photograph by John Bartelstone, 2015

RODNEY LEON

National Slavery Memorial in Washington, D.C.

INTERVIEW

First published in Yale's *Constructs*

Nina Rappaport
When you studied at Yale as a postprofessional, which professors most influenced and inspired you in general and also to explore African culture and find your own voice?

Rodney Leon
Going to Yale was a real thrill for me. I transferred from Pratt because of my interest in developing a culturally contextual design around the African diaspora. I had come across an exhibition curated by legendary art historian Robert Farris Thompson that explored the cultures of the African diaspora to a degree that I had never come across before. I wanted to look at things outside of architecture. I took Thompson's classes, French, and cultural studies. I was a member of NOMAS, which collaborated with artists, art historians, and film students to organize two different postcolonial film series and symposia. The professor that influenced me most was Eric Owen Moss because he challenged us in terms of our assumptions, intellectually and otherwise. I remember showing him a project for a museum in France, and he said, "Wow, why don't you just call I. M. Pei and call it a day?" Actually I loved Pei and worked for Sandi and Didi Pei after I graduated. So I proceeded through the rest of the semester doing things that I never thought I was going to do and came out with a completely different kind of project.

You have a Haitian background and you're working on projects there now, but did you ever visit Haiti when you were younger?

My parents and my wife's were born in Haiti and fled political persecution. They weren't keen on going back, even though at certain points they wished they could. So I grew up in a first-generation cultural experience that bridged two worlds. I started going to Haiti in my early twenties because my professor at Pratt, Gerard Paul, was Haitian. He worked for African-American architect Harry Simmons Jr., who was coarchitect with Philip Johnson on the AT&T building. Paul had a project in Haiti to renovate a theater and took me there.

Is that when your heritage became a focus in terms of design and cultural context? When did you start expressing those ideas in design projects or monuments?

As an African American I had an interest in how we explore creativity and cultural identity. I joined with fellow students at Yale, including a friend from the Ivory Coast with whom I worked later, to respond to an ideas competition for the African Burial Ground in New York City. We focused on ideas around memory and culture, but we didn't win.

Maya Lin was a young student at Yale ten years before when she entered the Vietnam Veterans War Memorial competition and won. Were you inspired by her determination and process?

I was inspired by the fact that she was so young and created this cosmic shift in the way people perceived memorialization and space.

What methods do you use to approach the design of a memorial site that is not just a wordy plaque on a wall? How do you approach something that's not there anymore but you want people to know about? How do you convey something ephemeral as a haptic and cultural experience—through light, sound, textures, and materials—as in your design for the African Burial Ground National Monument?

One of the things that helps coming up with a solution is the process itself. The fact that I have the freedom to reference different modes of communication in order to tell a story in as broad a way as possible is important. Words are one way of communicating, and then there are the spatial and the visual methods. You said you hate plaques; I hate plaques too because they are lazy. Memorials need to be spatial and interactive; you need to be able to move through elements like landscaping and water, a physical object in a natural environment. Material should lend a sense of permanence and transcend generations, to stay with you and exude a sense of the sacred. Often you are dealing with the memory of solemn historical conditions and experiences that are very real to people. I'm not interested in emphasizing actual suffering. I want to create environments in which one can reflect and find a hope for healing and transition rather than express shame, hate, sorrow, anger, or fear. A memorial

Rodney Leon, Ark of Return, New York, photograph by John Bartelstone, 2015

should be a healing object, almost like an amulet that you touch and then feel that you understand the significance of what happened as well as how to move through and live with it for future generations.

The African Burial Ground Memorial was made for a specific site, whereas the UN Memorial to Slavery, the Ark of Return, was not. They are different conceptually and thus show two directions for memorial design, one that is more universal and the other related to a location. How do you choose what to make visible and manifest it in an abstract way?

The Ark of Return had more limitations, such as a very small footprint, and I was trying to figure out how to maximize the user experience while benefiting from the scale of the plaza. Having this object at the end of the plaza, framed by the General Assembly Building on your right and the UN Rose Garden on your left, draws you to it, and the object helps to complete the space, acting as an extension of what's already there. The triangular oculus is illuminated and draws you in. The themes were to "acknowledge the tragedy, consider the legacy, lest we forget"—recognizing the history of the transatlantic slave trade as well as contemporary slavery. In some ways it's a sister monument to the burial ground, which creates a similar idea of passing through and transcendence. As a Catholic you go through the narthex of a church, a transitional space, before entering the sacred structure. The idea of the return and transformation is something we called the "door of return" in the burial ground, and then we created the Ark of Return. So there's a connected symbolism.

Why the sculpture of a human figure rather than an abstract form? How was it carved and to whose design?

I didn't even think about that, but it's an interesting question and something that I struggled with. We called it the trinity figure. We were trying to come up with a way to express the significance of the Middle Passage. The idea of that figure is to manifest the men, women, and children who were lost during that transatlantic passage. It's a spirit that is returning, hence the Ark of Return. I'm not a classicist at all, but I felt that there was something missing in terms of manifesting that spirit. I thought it would be nice to see a classical ebony figure draped in an elegant cloth as a spirit that's being taken back. I did a sketch and worked with sculptors who made mock-ups and hand-carved it. One sculptor carved the head, the hand, and the leg from black Zimbabwe granite and another sculpted the robe in white marble. When you look at that window you see the hand coming out and drawing you through. The figure helps to tell the story in a way that people can grasp easily.

How did Black Lives Matter and the focus on systemic racism affect your work? Was it a moment of change, intensity, or validation?

It's been very helpful because the country, and the world, is opening our eyes to hidden histories and opportunities to reevaluate who we are, where we come from, how we tell the story, and who gets to tell their story. It's a much more complex story than what we've been taught. And people are pushing back. Even before the George Floyd murder Mayor di Blasio put together a monument commission, and the protests encapsulated a lot of the frustrations. I think it's a very important opportunity right now for architects and artists to communicate that history to future generations in a

Rodney Leon, African Burial Ground, New York, photograph by John Bartelstone, 2007

way that is much more inclusive than it has been in the past. It's something that I find to be both challenging and problematic. How do you begin to change people's ideas about what memorialization is, what it represents, and how it can be communicated?

You have a related project now in Washington, D.C. What are the issues at the Mount Zion Cemetery in Georgetown?

Headstones at the cemetery were scattered all over the place. I was asked to do a master plan for two adjacent cemeteries—one is Mount Zion, which is related to the church, and the other is for the Female Union Band, a group of people from the community. A large African-American group banded together to take care of the site, so there was this historic rift, but now they're working more collaboratively on ways to memorialize and preserve the history.

Do you have any current projects that are inspiring ideas for cultural context and design?

I'm working with a group called Black Gotham Experience that gives tours of Manhattan about Black history. This past year we collaborated on a series of walking tours with the National Park Service and the Lower Manhattan Cultural Council during its River To River Festival. We are trying to illuminate the significant roles people of African descent played in the development of New York City. The location of the eighteenth-century African slave market has just a small plaque that was erected in 2015. That's obviously quite underwhelming. There is a lot to be learned and explored about providing opportunities for people to reflect on the history and understand how New York City was transformed.

What are you teaching at Yale?

In the Fall I was an advisor for Phil Bernstein's seminar on slavery and the built environment. Now I am teaching a studio on a national slavery memorial in Washington, D.C. It's not a real competition, but there are people working toward trying to find a site and propose legislation for implementing it as a national project.

ESSAY

National Slavery Memorial in Washington, D.C.

Society is undergoing reevaluation of many social constructs and traditions once understood to be established normative points of reference. This is especially true in regard to historic definitions and our understanding of issues related to race and gender. Our expanded awareness has triggered a transformation of the language we use to communicate to acknowledge the complexity, range, and fluidity of experiences and identities that comprise the human condition.

These changes have engendered tremendous social, political, and cultural debate played out across a variety of sectors in business, law, government, history, education, and architecture. Most dramatically, many of our prominent and historic public spaces have become places of contestation for citizens to challenge systems of oppression and prevailing exclusive historic narratives. As a result, many of these public spaces—and the memorials, monuments, and historic markers that define them—are undergoing significant transformations.

One of the major responsibilities of architects, designers, and artists is to give physical form through memorials to abstract ideas that reflect our common values and aspirations. Considering what is happening nationally we must ask ourselves, "Does the current memorial landscape truly reflect a balanced, accurate, and inclusive narrative of the people, events, and movements that shaped our society?" If not, how can we as architects design places of memory that provide more honest, inclusive, and accurate representations of parts of our history that have been hidden, erased, lost, forgotten, or omitted? In his book *Silencing the Past: Power and the Production of History*, anthropologist Michel-Rolph Trouillot refers to these significant historical erasures as "silences."

The preeminent place where American collective national identity and shared values are given form is the National Mall, in Washington, D.C., where the most prominent monuments are those to Washington, Jefferson, and Lincoln—reflecting the values of independence, democracy, and freedom. In this context, arguably, the greatest "silence" on the National Mall is the absence of acknowledgment of the institution of slavery, the role it played in the formation of our nation, the impact it has had on the lives of the enslaved and their descendants, and the legacies it has left that we continue to struggle with as a society. The National Slavery Memorial studio proposed to address this tragic omission by transforming the memorial landscape of our nation's capital and constructing a historical narrative more reflective of our collective history and identity as citizens of the United States. The resulting design process is intended to serve as a resource for current and future legislative efforts by government and community stakeholders to build a memorial to slavery in Washington, D.C.

The design studio explored themes expressed by the title "Architecture of Resistance, Memory, and Resilience," considering the following key questions:

How can the students propose new formal expressions as alternatives to the traditional classical Confederate statuary, sculpture, and temples that society is most familiar with?

How can the students go beyond pure abstraction to create interactive and engaging spaces?

How can the students meaningfully contextualize the history of slavery in the United States using cultural traditions as a source of inspiration?

How can the students create opportunities for design and construction processes that are "restorative," providing acknowledgment and agency to those impacted by slavery and its ongoing legacy; and "reparative," introducing design and construction techniques that create economic, cultural, social, and educational opportunities, along with equitable conditions for inclusion of descendant communities?

Learning objectives for the students focused on the following seven areas of inquiry.

1 Historical Contextualization

The studio utilized research, mapping, and analysis to identify historic omissions and erasures related to slavery from the public consciousness and then investigated strategies to reveal, expand our understanding of, and contextualize them in our collective history.

2 Cultural Contextualization

The studio identified intangible forces of culture in the African-American community to employ as materiality for the construction of places of memory. Elements of music, dance, art, ritual, religion, social practices, and language were used to inspire spaces intrinsically connected to and reflective of descendant communities.

3 Architectural Narration

Students identified themes and developed written narratives to tell stories reflecting historic experiences as the basis for memorialization.

4 Architecture Language

Given that the memorial landscape of Washington, D.C., is dominated by figurative sculpture and classical architecture, students were asked to establish a set of rules or organizing principles comprising a new architectural taxonomy and language that challenges, engages, or complements the prevailing formal and visual order.

5 Community Engagement

Students created a set of design goals and objectives with input from stakeholders and descendant communities. This engagement was critical to the spirit of creating an inclusive monument process that reflects the aspirations of communities that historically have been excluded.

6 Interactive Space

The studio attempted to invert the notion of a monument or memorial as being a static object to be seen and admired from a distance. Students were challenged to create spaces to be engaged by users through physical and ritual interaction and movement.

7 Restorative Justice

Students explored ways in which the planning, design, and construction process could be restorative and reparative. They also imagined opportunities for engagement, education, and training as well as for healing local descendant communities and society at large.

STUDIO BRIEF

National Slavery Memorial Design Studio

The National Slavery Memorial design studio served as the basis for redefining the memorial landscape and, in turn, the historical narrative of our collective identity as citizens of the United States. The result of the studio design process may serve as a resource for ongoing efforts by the government and community stakeholders to establish a more equitable landscape of memory within our nation's capital and for legislative efforts to build a memorial to slavery in Washington, D.C.

The studio was an extension of the ongoing interdisciplinary collaborative research seminar Problem Solving Initiative (PSI) entitled "Slavery, Its Legacies, and the Built Environment," organized by Yale School of Architecture, Yale Law School, the Gilder Lehrman Center, and University of Michigan Law School. The fall seminar was led by Phil Bernstein, professor at Yale School of Architecture, and Luis C. deBaca, professor at the University of Michigan Law School. Yale University historian David Blight and architect Rodney Leon acted as advisors. The PSI group seminar produced a comprehensive 400-page Narrative Framework Document for the "National Slavery Memorial" design studio. The document investigated the phenomenon of slavery through the lenses of law, history, architecture, and systems of labor with the goal of constructing environments free of human exploitation. In Spring 2022 students from the seminar established an Advanced PSI Consultancy Group to serve as both a resource and a critical partner for YSoA students, who read, analyzed, and prepared concepts for review and discussion with the group throughout the semester. Ultimately the YSoA studio design work was integrated as part of an edited Enhanced Framework Document (EFD). The research outlined in the EFD became a valuable resource for the students' process of absorbing and engaging the complex, expansive topic in a short period of time.

The course emphasized the design process through both individual and collective activity. The initial phase of the semester explored the history of slavery through readings, discussions, presentations, and writing. The students investigated the concept of memorialization by examining precedents and analyzed the historic landscape of the site through mapping and analysis.

The proposed site for the memorial is located in a zone occupied by two large underutilized sections of West Potomac Park within the southern portion of a zone established by the National Park Service known as the Area 1 Reserve. The area is currently established as the monumental core of Washington, D.C., and no additional memorials are allowed to be built. For purposes of the design studio the restriction was suspended to allow students the opportunity to engage a site in proximity to the National Mall. We also felt strongly that it would be a disservice to the historic significance of the subject to propose a site outside of the national monumental core. The absence of a National Slavery Memorial in the monumental core is a continuation of a legacy of neglect and omission of the most profound tragedy in our nation's history. The proposed site's proximity to the Tidal Basin and the Potomac River, as well as its urban relationship to the national monuments to significant leaders and wars, was ideal for inspiring the students to conceive of memorial designs on a grand scale.

Initial Project

The prominent site and complex topic warranted an introductory two-week design assignment. The students were asked to create a place

of memory for Georgetown's historic Mount Zion and Female Union Band Society Cemeteries as an exploration of the topic of slavery in memory and history at a smaller scale. The initial project emphasized the theme "Freedom Quilt" as the inspiration for a "transformative memorial landscape." The process of physical transformation was inspired by patterns, geometries, and techniques used by enslaved African Americans to construct the so-called "freedom quilts": collaborative, intergenerational artifacts of memory often embedded with histories, coded messages, and meanings that served as subtle forms of resistance. Students were encouraged and inspired by the history of the Underground Railroad and readings from *Narrative of the Life of Frederick Douglass, an American Slave*. Many of their projects and narratives referenced themes of movement, escape, concealment, and shelter.

Selected Examples of Student Cemetery Projects

Adam Rostek's "Cloak of Zion" explores the qualities of the freedom quilt as a system of stitched components, emphasizing the points of intersection between each segment as the connective tissue within an arrangement of dynamic elements. These contextualize the quilt within the site by drawing an analogy between its undulating fabric and the severe hillside topography. The arrangement creates an experiential relationship between the flowing quality of the patchwork and the sloping land. The movement of an existing footpath through the site, from southwest to northeast, is reinforced by a meandering route with adjacent spaces varying in scale anchored by enlightening beacons of subjective information.

A rigid perimeter frame contrasts the fluidity of the interior figural arrangement, where human interaction with a cruciform column varies in intensity based on the height of the vertical extrusion. Movement through the site entails a sequential shift of spatial characteristics employing materials of the extracted points on stitch intersections, changing from opaque to transparent, heavy to light, uncomfortable to peaceful, concrete to ethereal.

April Liu's "Crossroads" references the so-named pattern in freedom quilts that evokes a main crossroads in Cleveland, Ohio, where there were several routes toward freedom. On a less literal level, it also reflects the meaning of the term *crossroads* as a turning point in one's life, where a significant choice must be made. A circle, a nondirectional shape, is inserted into the center of a crossroads, offering an open-minded choice during a difficult journey. The manipulation of the landscape evokes the material quality of a quilt. Soft and undulating, the memorial structure is submerged partially into the terrain to be revealed only as one approaches it. Hidden pathways lined by walls with marble plaques reflect the secrecy of a freedom quilt as a tool of resistance and an object of remembrance.

Studio Travel

Martin Luther King Jr. Memorial, Washington, D.C.

The studio travel itinerary included trips to historic sites in the South that have been transformed recently to engage the complexity of their historic relationships with the institution of slavery through the design of public and cultural spaces. Students first traveled to Montgomery, Alabama, to visit the National Memorial for Peace and Justice and the Legacy Museum. The second stop was Charlottesville, Virginia, to tour the University of Virginia campus and the Memorial to Enslaved Laborers. The highlight of a private tour of Thomas Jefferson's Monticello was a discussion with a descendant of Sally Hemings. The last stop was Washington, D.C., to document the memorial's proposed waterfront site in West Potomac Park, between the Potomac River and the Tidal Basin just south of the Lincoln and Martin Luther King Jr. Memorials. The class also toured memorials and monuments on the National Mall as well as the National Museum of African American History and Culture.

Equal Justice Initiative office, in Montgomery, Alabama

Cabin of enslaved worker, Monticello, Charlottesville, Virginia

First-floor interior, Monticello, Charlottesville, Virginia

Upper-level interior, Monticello, Charlottesville, Virginia

National Memorial for Peace and Justice, Montgomery, Alabama

Monticello, Charlottesville, Virginia

University of Virginia, Charlottesville, Virginia

University of Virginia, Charlottesville, Virginia

National Museum of African American History and Culture and the Washington Monument, Washington, D.C.

Jefferson Memorial, Washington, D.C.

Memorial to Enslaved Laborers, University of Virginia, Charlottesville, Virginia

Jefferson Memorial, Washington, D.C.

Community Engagement

In Washington, D.C., the students had the unique opportunity to receive public input on the concept of a National Slavery Memorial at a community-engagement workshop organized by the Black Georgetown Foundation at the historic Dumbarton House. Featuring presentations by National Park Service superintendent Julia Washburn and U.S. Congresswoman Eleanor Holmes Norton, the event was attended by approximately 40 leaders representing a broad cross section of stakeholders primarily from nonprofit, government, and education sectors, including architecture students from Howard University.

The goal was for the memorial design process to incorporate aspirations of descendant communities aligned with values of restorative justice. The workshop provided the students with an interactive venue to listen to the voices and opinions of local community stakeholders. A series of community recommendations emerged from those listening sessions, allowing the students to go back to their studios at Yale and prepare design proposals incorporating vital community input.

Community-engagement workshop held at Dumbarton House, Georgetown, Washington, D.C.

Objectives

Upon returning from their travels, the students were asked to explore how they could design memorials that

> **Propose alternative new formal approaches to the traditional language of monuments and memorials we are most familiar with.**
>
> **Create more opportunities and spaces that encourage physical interaction and engagement.**
>
> **Contextualize the history of slavery in the United States in a meaningful way, particularly using cultural traditions as a source of inspiration.**
>
> **Create opportunities through design and construction processes that are "restorative" by providing acknowledgment and agency to those impacted by slavery and its ongoing legacy, and "reparative" by producing economic, cultural, social, and educational opportunities along with equitable conditions for descendant communities.**
>
> **Address and support goals and aspirations outlined in the community-engagement forum and the PSI framework document.**

STUDENT WORK

April Liu

Michelle Qu

Shiqi Li

Jingyuan Qiu

Quincy Ding

Fan Yang

Rosa Congdon

Adam Rostek

Mingxi Li

Janell Schmidt

April Liu

Safe Haven: National Slavery Memorial

Architecture of Resistance: The Maroon Community

Throughout the history of enslaved laborers, different resistance tools emerged to support, nurture, and demand freedom. The institution of slavery was threatened when large groups of enslaved Africans escaped to geographically secluded regions in the Americas to form runaway societies, often referred to as Maroon communities. They developed a culture, government, system of trade, and military defense against their European and American oppressors.

Site Strategy

The site is organized as a series of islands that evoke Maroon communities. Passages below the water stitch together scattered pieces of memory, connecting people to the nation's past and history. The underutilized road along the Potomac River is eliminated, and traffic is rerouted around the site. As a fluid, restorative, and consistent element throughout the site, water is brought in from the Potomac River through a double-layered filtering system. The first layer of breakwater symbolizes a historic slave-trade port transformed into a place for reflection. The tragic history depicted below the surface of the water is revealed only when the water is drained on certain meaningful dates, including Emancipation Day (April 16), Juneteenth (June 19), and off-work days for enslaved people (Sundays). At the tip of the central island is a hidden Maroon village, a haven protected by a perimeter defense hosting a museum and gathering grounds.

Site plan showing primary reflecting-pool condition with full water level

Site plan showing primary reflecting-pool condition half-full of water

Site plan showing primary reflecting pool condition with no water

Topographic site model

Detail model of exhibition pavilions

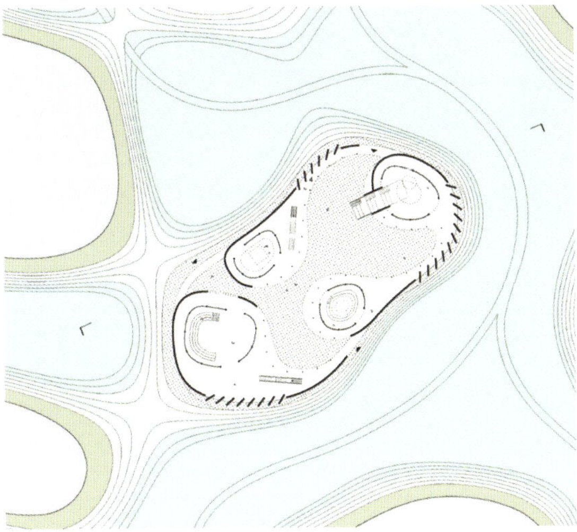

Ground-floor plan

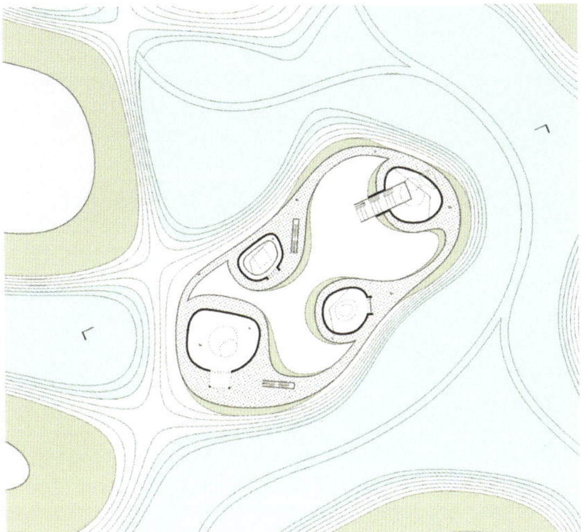

Second-floor plan

Longitudinal cross section

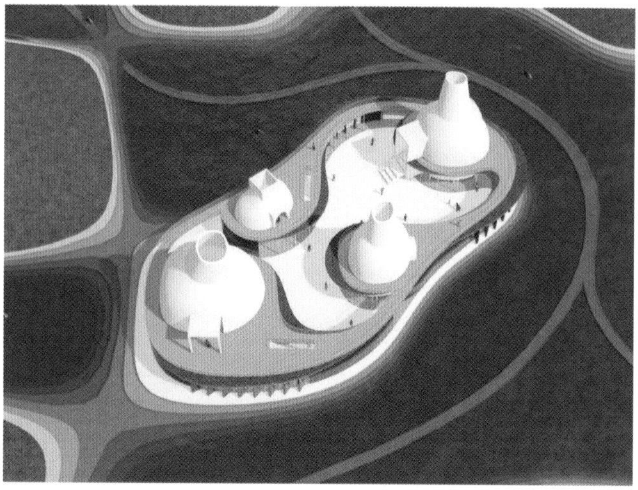

Aerial view

Pavilion with oculus view to Washington Monument

Interior courtyard

Michelle Qu

The Contradictory Site

The United States has a deeply conflictual and highly contradictory narrative. The nation's promotion of the ideal of "life, liberty, and the pursuit of happiness" is directly opposed by its history of slavery, which is essentially absent from the narrative and landscape of memorialization.

How could Washington, D.C., a former hub of the slave trade where people were bought and sold, be the seat of our government and symbol of our morals while the legacy of suffering and sacrifice of the enslaved people on whose backs the city was built is yet to be genuinely acknowledged? Placing the capital in this location ensured that slavery was ingrained into every aspect of life, including the buildings, institutions, and social fabric of the city.

Triangular Trade

Beginning in the sixteenth century and lasting until the early nineteenth century, a commercial relationship formed across the Atlantic Ocean, based mainly on the slave trade. Taking place between Africa, America, and Europe, the exchange route came to be known as the "triangular trade." As a commodity, enslaved people were forced to endure a brutal three-month journey to America on what became known as the Middle Passage.

Memorial Design

This memorial looks to contextualize the contradictions in the history of Washington, D.C., and America. A tilted, broken triangle, which resembles a sinking vessel, symbolizes the revelation of truth in the context of the above-ground void, used as a space for the celebration of freedom, while the underground space reflects the darkness of history and an aspiration for hope and light.

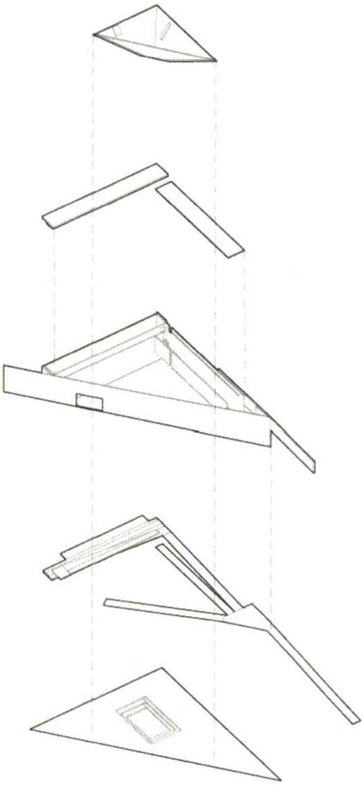

Isometric projection of court, circulation ramps, enclosure, roof terrace, and inverted pyramid void

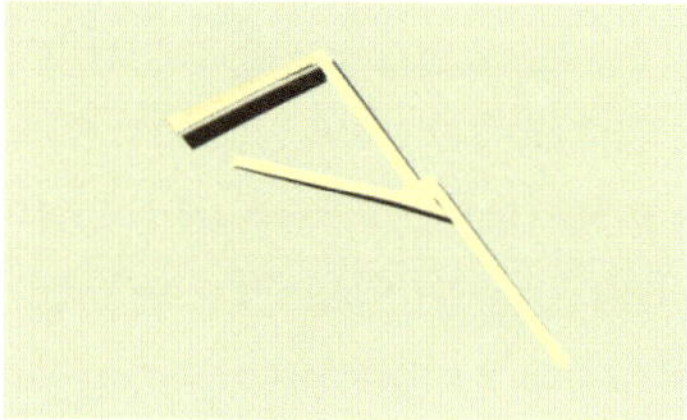

Isometric projection of circulation ramps

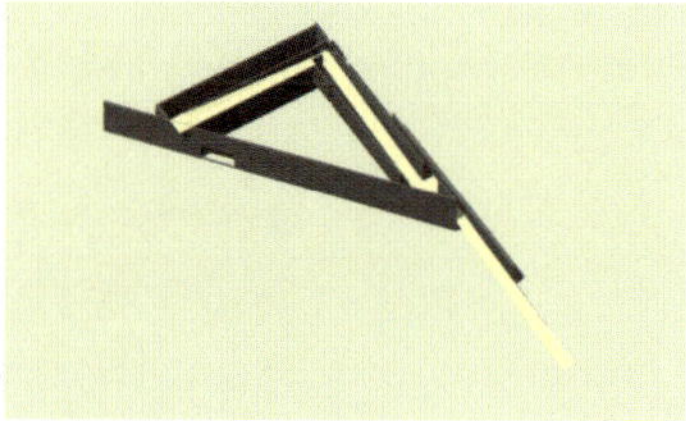

Isometric projection of circulation ramps and enclosure

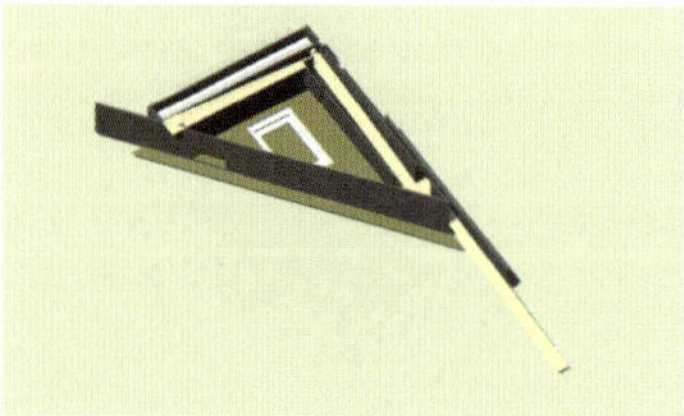

Isometric projection of circulation ramps, enclosure, and court

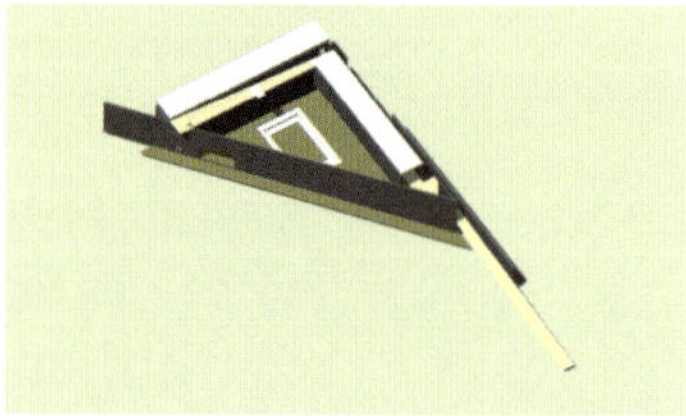

Isometric projection of circulation ramps, enclosure, court, and roof terrace

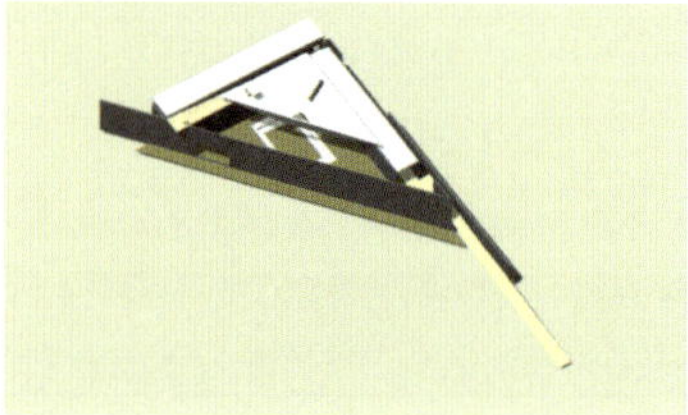

Isometric projection of circulation ramps, enclosure, court, roof terrace, and inverted pyramid void

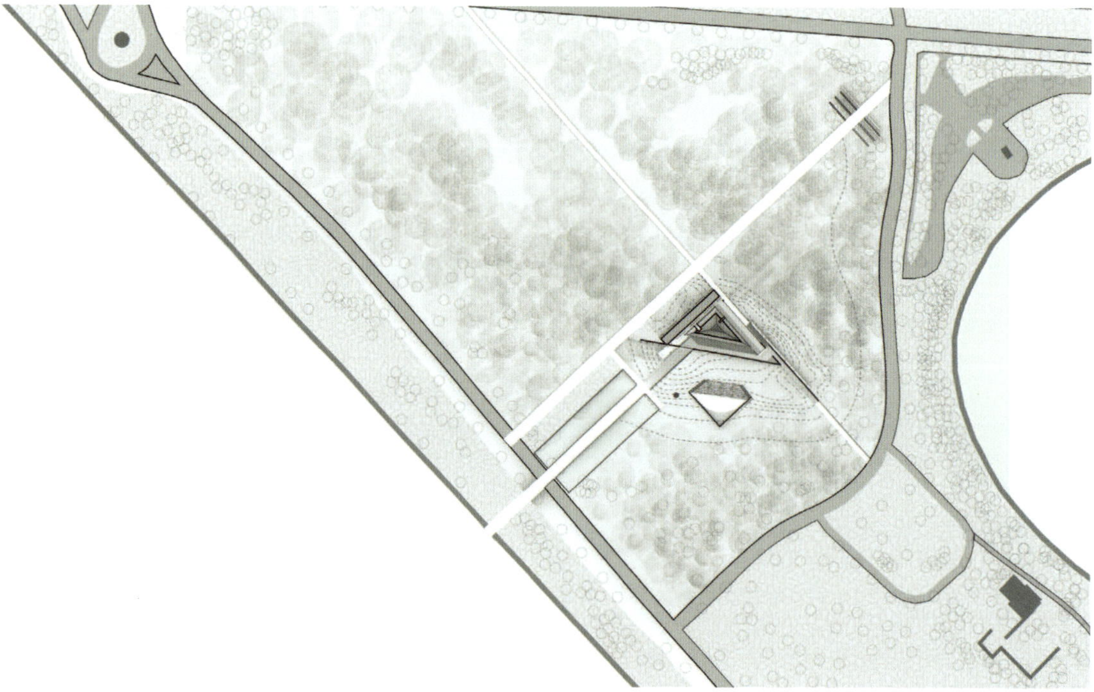

Site plan

Interior of court with inverted pyramidal oculus

Exterior from the roof terrace with view of the Washington and Jefferson Memorials

Exterior of the void

Shiqi Li

Slavery Did Not End; It Evolved.

Slavery is not a past-tense history but an unsolved predicament that is constantly evolving. A slavery memorial should not only reflect the past but also confront the challenging aspects of the present to catalyze a restorative engagement for the future. The project proposes three spatial conditions echoing the different periods of slavery to provoke a transformative experience through concealing and revealing, ascending and descending, darkness and brightness.

The Chapter of the Past: 1501–1865

The space of the past is a chapel, emphasizing the origin of slavery. Descending into a space below the water recalls the voyage of the transatlantic slave trade, while a wooden chamber with cracks allowing light to enter echoes the darkness of slave-ship hulls. Marble headstones interpret the scale and layout of ship packing, and a black river stone provides a ground for mourning the lives lost at the bottom of the ocean.

The Chapter of the Present: 1865–present

A maze reflects slavery's evolved present form, interpreting the meandering journey of reconstruction. Cor-Ten steel screens leaning both forward and backward represent the barriers to freedom and the people who fight back.

The Chapter of the Future

The space of the future is a vertical cemetery commemorating the unrecognized heroes in the ongoing fight for freedom and justice. It is also an incubator for community engagement and restorative events. As walnut caskets with the ashes of pioneers are being claimed, the niche is filled with glass panels engraved with the names of previous occupants. Thus over time the columbarium will transform from a dim enclosed space to a light-filled memorial.

Exterior entrance view of Pavilion of the Past

Cross-section view of Pavilion of the Past

Interior of Pavilion of the Past

Interior of Pavilion of the Present
(perpendicular to translucent screens)

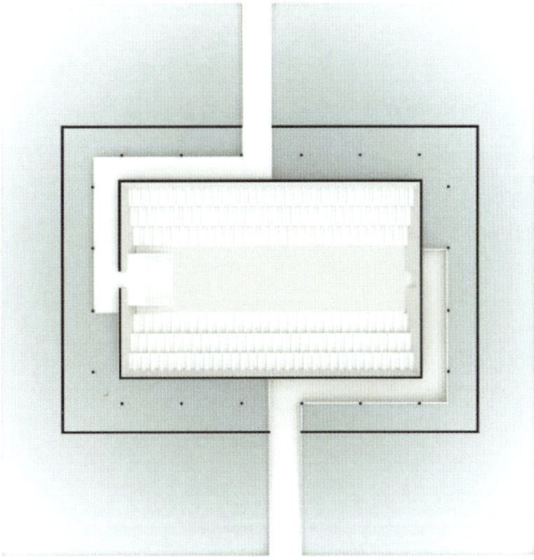

Plan of Pavilion of the Past

Exterior side view of Pavilion of the Past (area adjacent to reflecting pool)

Interior of Pavilion of the Present
(parallel to translucent screens)

Entrance to Pavilion of the Future

Interior of Pavilion of the Future (lower level)

Interior of Pavilion of the Future (upper level)

Jingyuan Qiu

Underground Railroad

Slavery is America's open wound. It is the painful injury that 13 percent of Americans live with and the rest of the country attempts to ignore because, for them, it is an ancient scar. The very term *slavery* evokes emotions so strong that many Americans no longer speak of it, while others who live with its enduring impact cry it aloud in hopes that the country will finally have the conversation it has refused to have for nearly 400 years. The primary goal of this National Memorial of Slavery is to provide a healing space for conversations that commemorate this history and a public park honoring the resiliency of African Americans.

Site Strategy

The project's proposed topography forms an hourglass shape. Two long hills represent massive scars in the landscape and separate the site into two zones, the north and the south. The space between the hills extends along the east-west axis, visually connecting the Abraham Lincoln and Franklin Delano Roosevelt Memorials. This "Valley of Freedom" is intended as a place to heal the open wound, and moving through it represents the historic journey from slavery to freedom.

Underground Railroad

The Underground Railroad was an extensive interconnected network of people and places that helped fugitive enslaved people make their way to freedom by providing shelter, money, transportation, food, clothing, goods, and legal services. The project reinterprets the system as a labyrinth of pathways and rooms constructed to convey the journey of escape. Entrances are embedded in the hillside along the north and south faces, but the end of these pathways is unknown—and at times the path unfolds as a dead-end. Other pathways lead to the other side of the hill and into the Valley of Freedom.

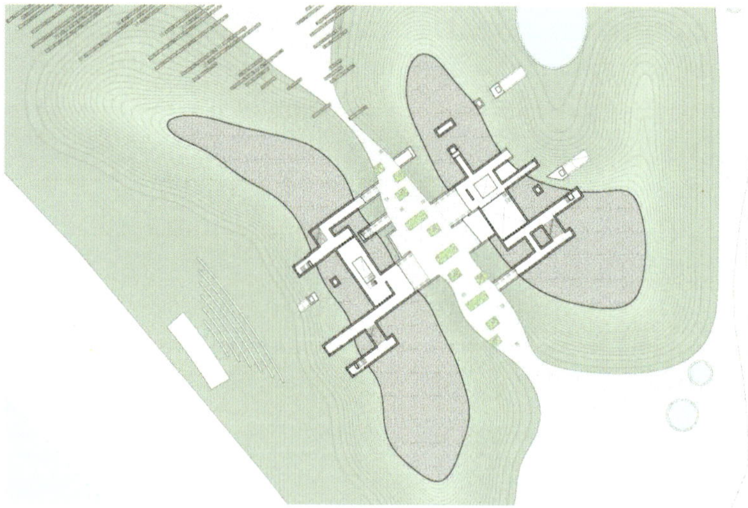

Level-one plan

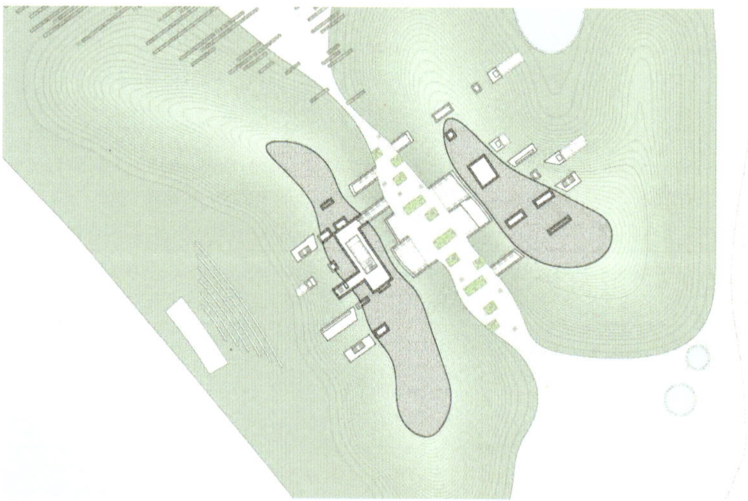

Level-two plan

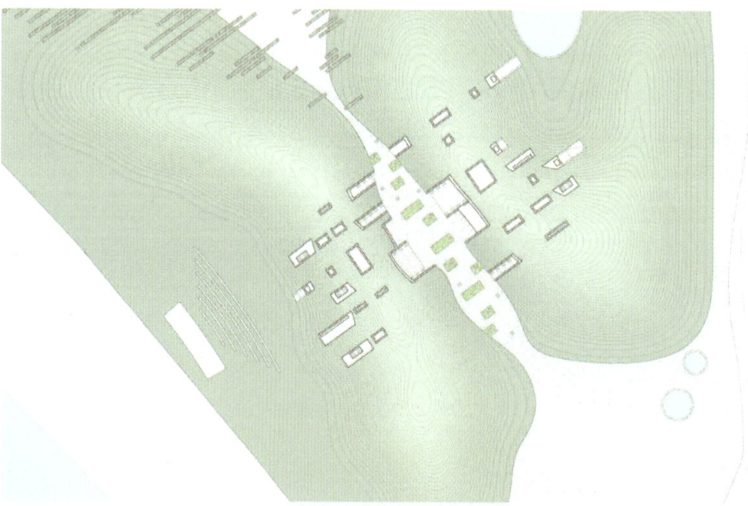

Level-three plan

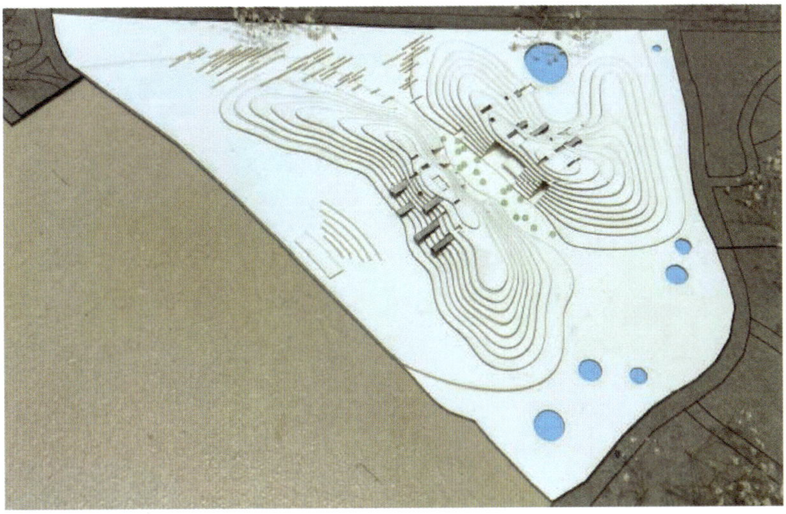

Site model

Exterior of southern mounds and terraces facing the Potomac River

Exterior of southern mounds and terraces looking north

Exterior of "Freedom Plaza" between north and south mounds looking west toward the Lincoln Memorial

Exterior at top of mound looking east toward Jefferson Memorial

Exterior of "Freedom Plaza" between north and south mounds looking east toward the Tidal Basin

Quincy Ding

Shadowed Land

This project is generated from two types of geometry. The first is the shape of a shadow, with brutal edges symbolizing horror and suffering, leaving visitors alienated. The second is a collection of perfect Platonic geometries—triangle, circle, rectangle—corresponding through abstraction, respectively, with the Washington Monument, Jefferson Memorial, and Lincoln Memorial. The former presidents represent the establishment of the United States, the creation of the Constitution, and the abolition of slavery.

Similarly the ideal geometries represent the goals of independence, freedom, and democracy. Made of white marble, they have a material connection to the traditional monumental buildings around the site. However, they also signal contradictions within these ideals since the United States was built on slavery, whose abolition led to the Civil War and whose shadow has remained in the discrimination issues of today.

Project Walk-Through

A sloping triangular plane forms the monument's entrance, suggesting pressure, sinking, and aberration as the visitor moves downward. The first chamber houses an exhibition hall. Passing through it, one arrives at the amphitheater, with seats and stage to the left and right. In the plaza three meters below ground level is a reflection pool, forcing visitors to walk along the surrounding walls and exit up to face the Potomac River.

Choosing to remain within the monument's bounds, one arrives at another exhibition space below the main fragment. The space overlaps partly with a circular plane, sloping upward, allowing visitors to travel along the side walls of the circle and finally reach the top, where a smaller circular reflecting pool allows for rest and reflection at the end of the trip.

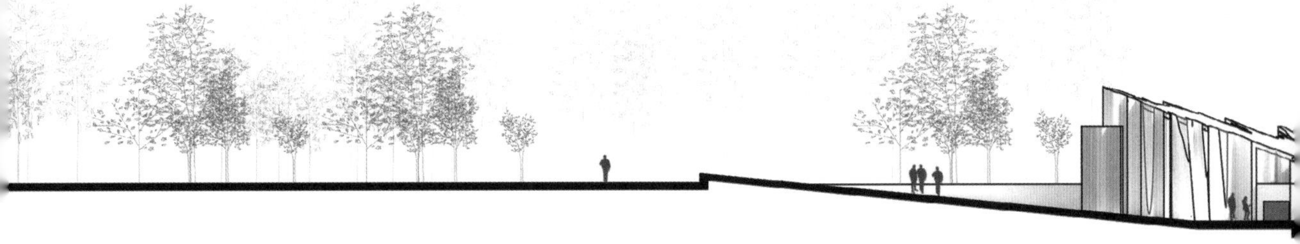

Section drawings

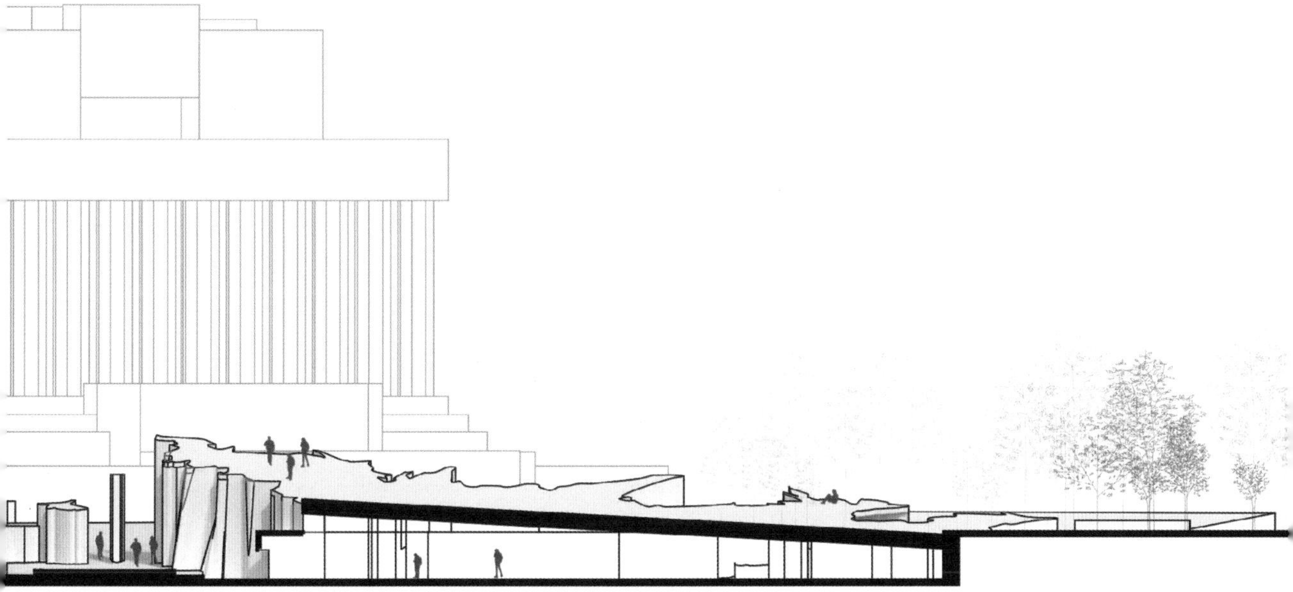

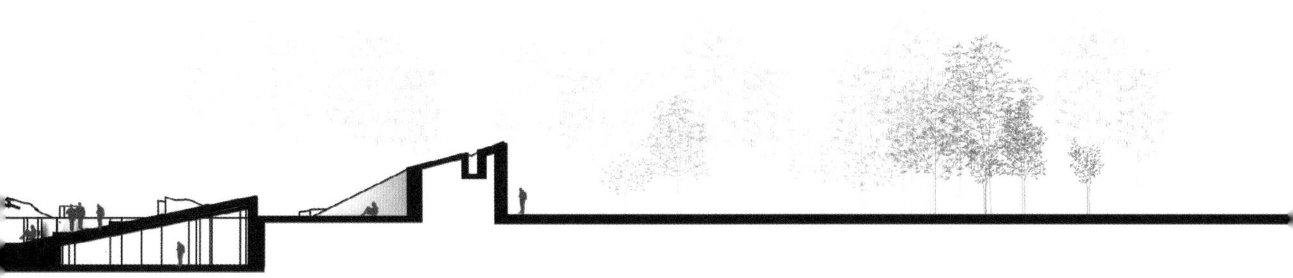

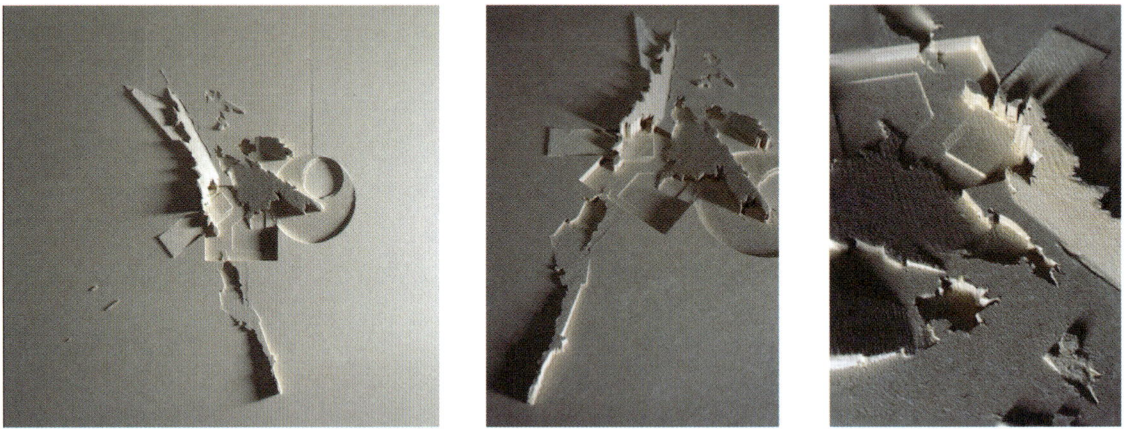

Topographical models

Initial drawings exploring abstract forms of the prototype

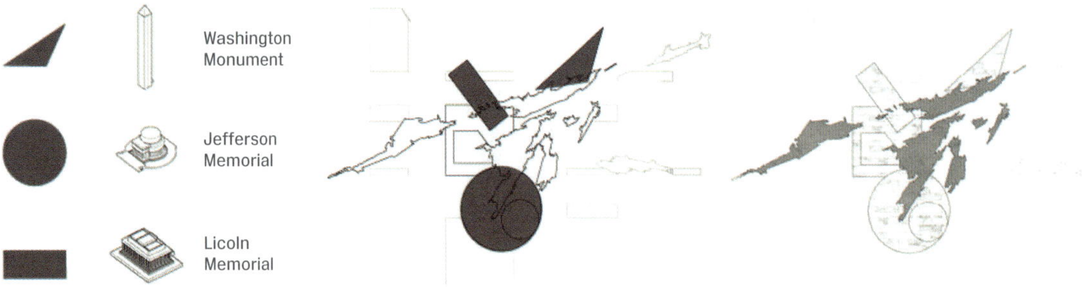

Metaphorical relationships to the existing monuments in Washington

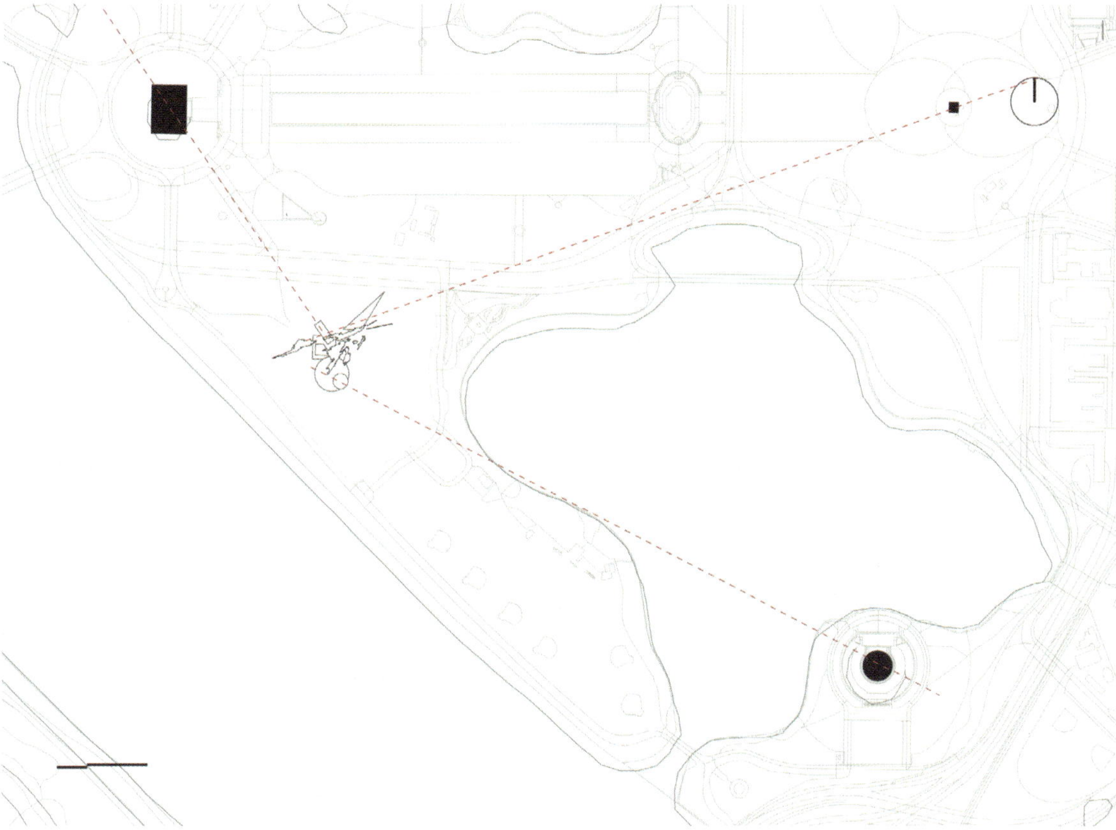

Site plan showing relationships to the other monuments

Perspective of the amphitheater

Perspective of the entrance to the exhibition hall

Perspective of exterior

Perspective of exterior

Fan Yang

The Stories of Pillars

In this project cubic stone pillars represent individual characters from slavery's history. The first one attempts to express the moral consequences of slavery from two perspectives—a secondhand observer and a firsthand witness—with the idea of inequality depicted through groups of columns with identical footprints but differing scales. The second part relates to landscape elements for reflection and commemoration, including a water wall, meditation platform, amphitheater, and basin arranged around the courtyard, the terrace, and the tunnel.

A gorge is cut into the middle of the site, aligned with the Washington Monument obelisk, piling up terrain on both sides. A second axis is generated by extending the path from the Lincoln Memorial across the gorge, symbolizing a national wound. The scheme allows the visitor to observe the gorge, first from high ground and then down inside of it, to experience the concealed and forgotten stories as a witness. Within the gorge the gradual shift from light to dark symbolizes the journey and struggle of the victims, with buttresses and trees along the edges representing lost souls. Streams of water flow down along each buttress, inspiring the gorge's name: Valley of Tears.

Site plan of gorge

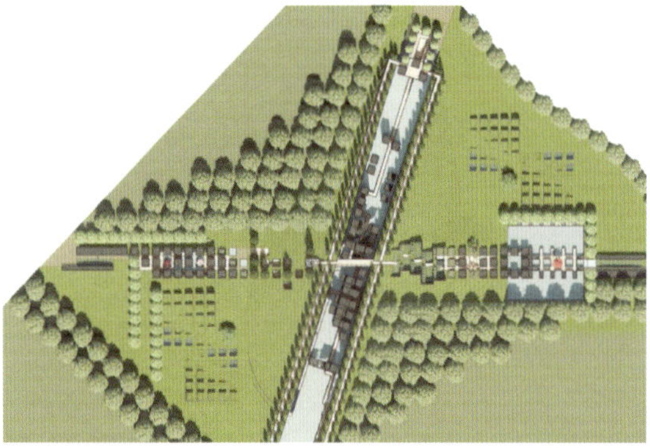

Site plan

Aerial view looking north

Memorial landscape at northeast corner of site looking west

Site model

Aerial view into the gorge

Interior of gorge looking north

Interior of gorge reflecting pool and walkways

Interior of gorge retaining wall, reflecting pool, and walkways

Exterior showing upper-level east reflecting pools looking west

Rosa Congdon

Memorial Landscape

The nation's enslavement history is embedded inextricably in the very physical landscape from where this democratic experiment was developed and disseminated. America's birth and growth is owed to the fertile land tilled by hand under the cruel circumstances of forced labor. The same hands crafted an America that, given the fault lines and failures implicit in this country, provided voices of hope though indelibility, perseverance, and resistance. These voices set off on a course through which we are still traveling to achieve equity, respect, love, justice, and peace. The land itself, a stolen gift of economic promise, was intimately experienced by people who were denied not only the profit from their relationship with the land but the consideration of basic humanity.

This memorial seeks to be a vessel for stories of enslaved people told throughout the American terrain—woven, unraveled, and rewoven in unique strands. The site receives pressure on its northern edge from Washington's memorial landscape, carrying visitors through a network of intersections toward the banks of the Potomac River. The landscape will make patterns of shelter and exposure, extending open rows of scarred paths up into an elevated canopy. The river is to be routed in bands crossing below the sloping canopy into a space defined by the edges of Independence Avenue and the Potomac. This way the memorial looks to recontextualize the land under American slavery, defining regions as vessels for personal narrative experiences while peeling cultivated land and layers of conscious erasure to unearth new spaces of truth.

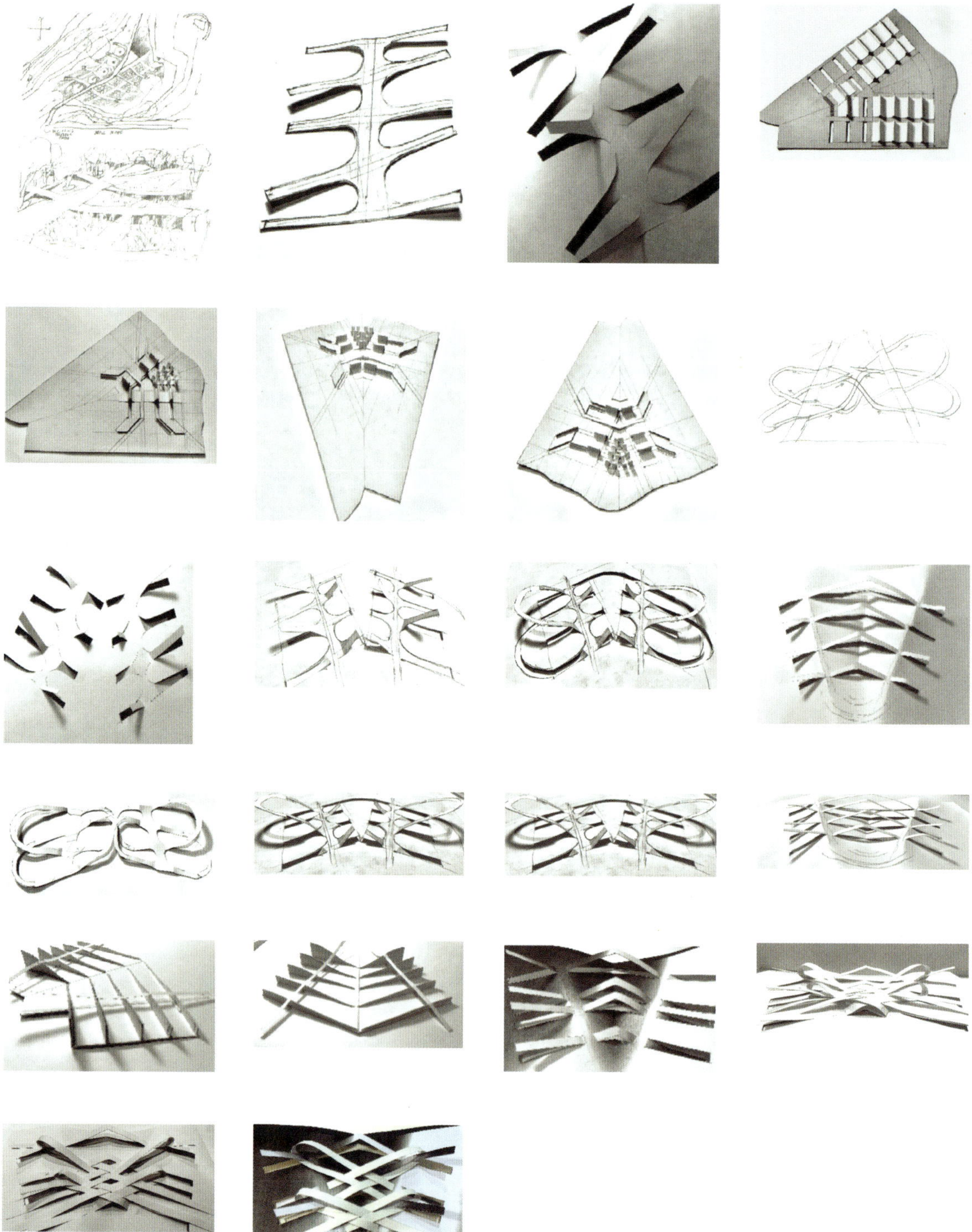

Study models of landscape weaves

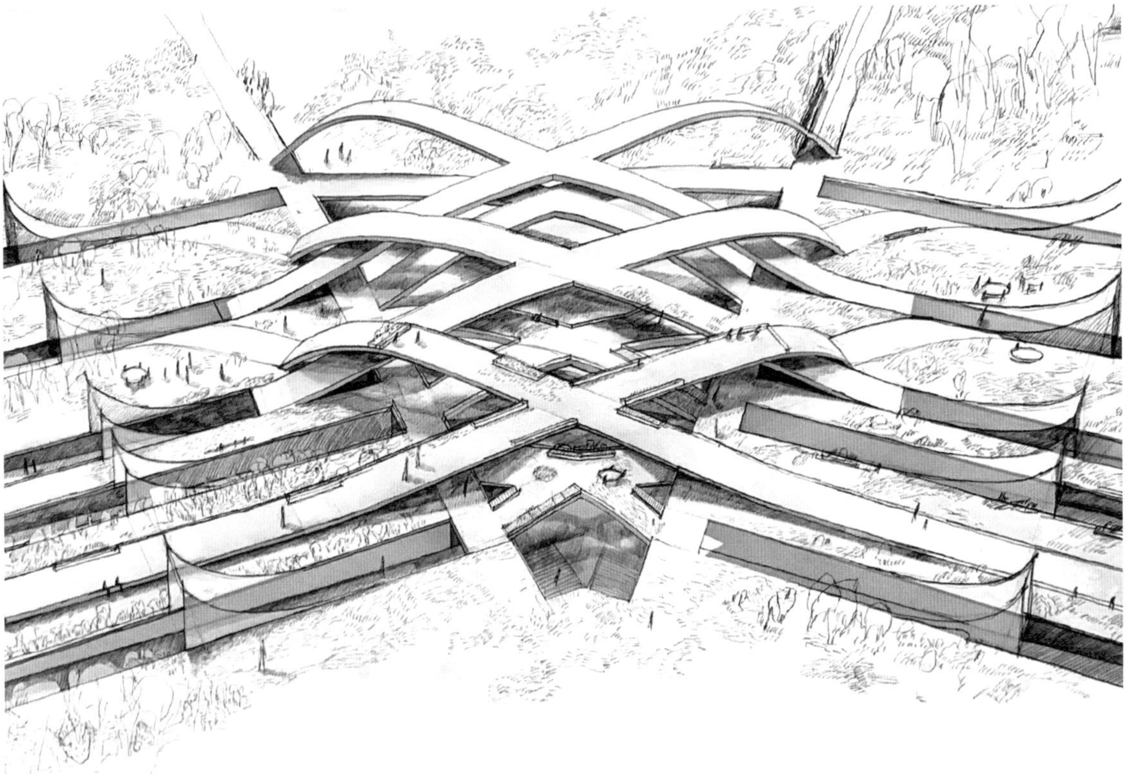

Aerial view of ramp and bridge gardens, graphite on paper

Study model collage on the Tidal Basin

Site plan of woven circulation from the National Mall to the Potomac River

Interior study, graphite on paper

Model of paths suturing the site

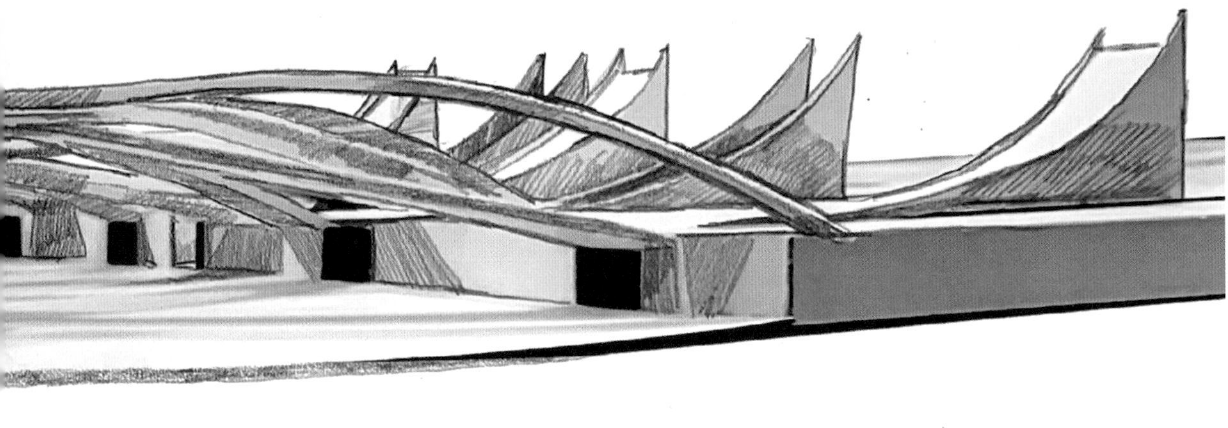

Adam Rostek

Scars of Reckoning

This project highlights the intersectionality of the ongoing repercussions of slavery and its deeply woven warps within the fabric of American culture. The physical manifestation of typological scars, just like their contextual repercussions, cut through to the core of American culture. Whether physical, social, geographical, or economic, the effects of slavery are still felt by descendants of those enslaved.

The project views the National Mall through historical, social, and political lenses, establishing a network of contextualized narratives forced into collision within the site, paralleling the Potomac River. The continuous material expression creates consistent yet dynamic movement between exterior and interior, exposing tensions, resolving conflicts of separate narratives, and forming a transformative experience across a hard, tangible line of an uncomfortable historical context. The conversation is set not simply through storytelling but also through story experiencing.

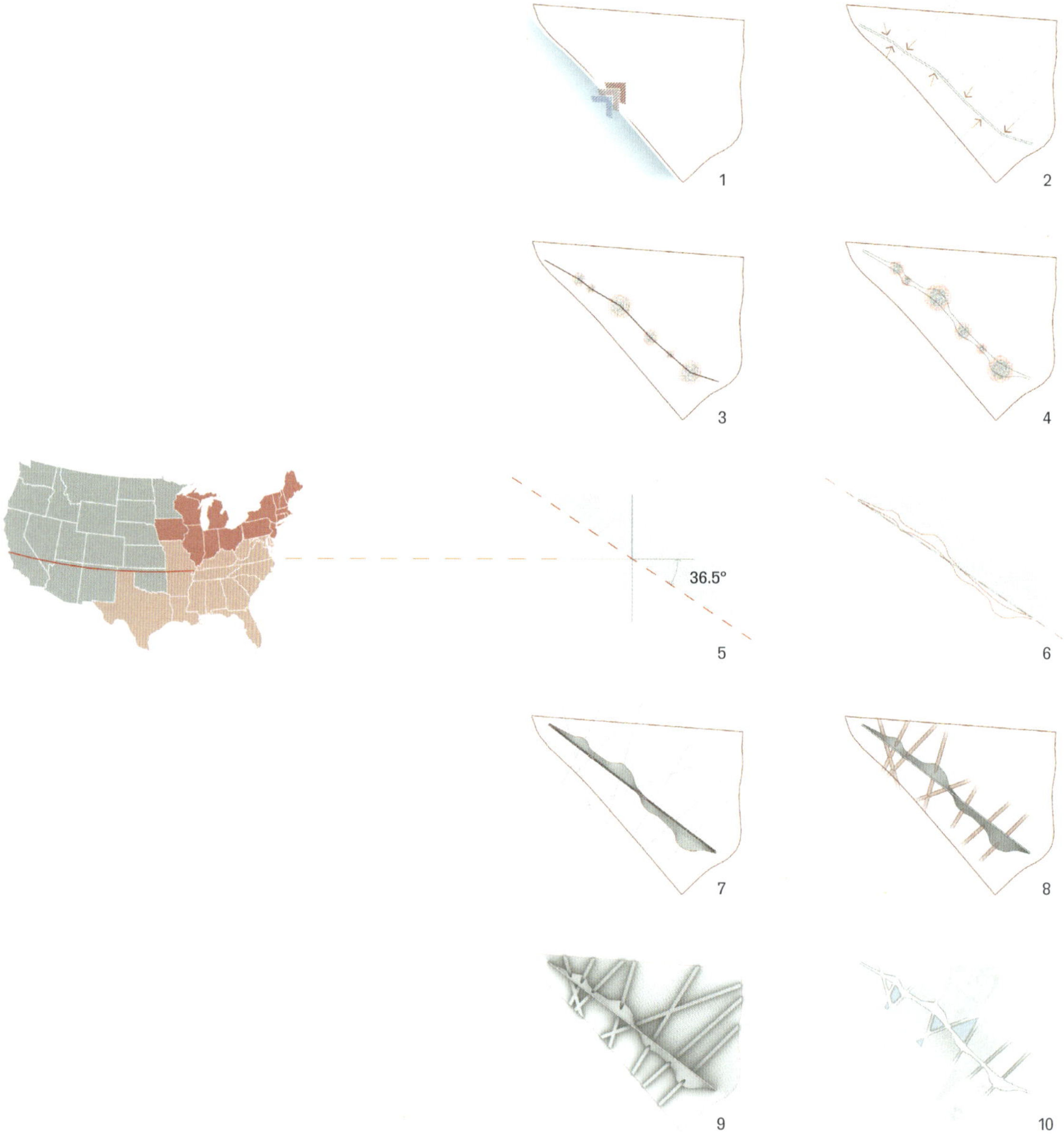

The Missouri Compromise line—the geographical separation between North and South established in 1820—translates its latitude line of 36 degrees and 30 minutes into the corresponding angle laid over the top of the fluid boundary of the structure.

The scale of the interior space compresses when the narrative darkens to force an intimate and intense atmospheric environment.

Creating a clear direction for the future narrative as a contrasting dialogue between North and South, the site provides a platform for reintroduction of the intersecting narratives within the footprint and their study as nodes of typological scars.

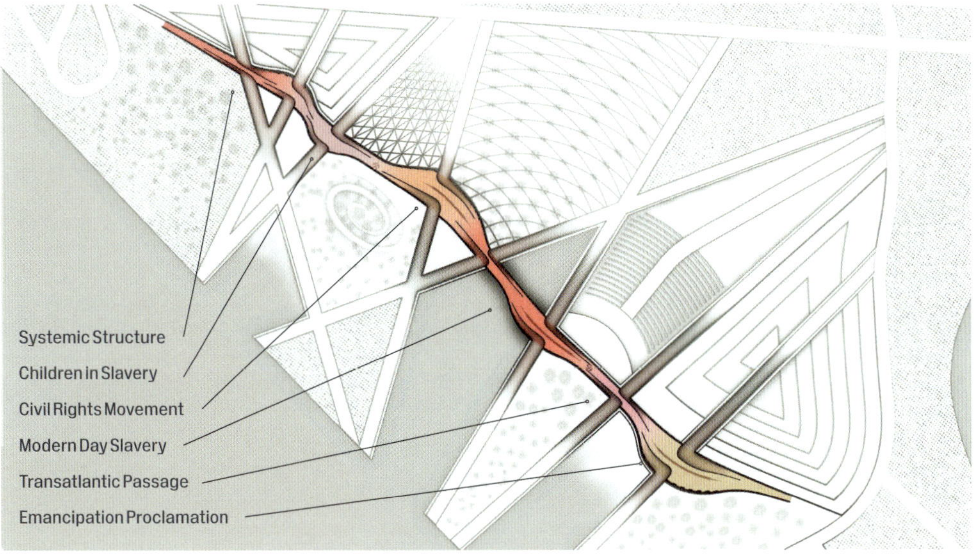

Nonlinear, nonchronological programmatic loading creates a story that develops through movement, where the shift between spaces creates tension, uncovers historical context, and suggests reconciliation.

The spatial quality of the interior expands when its accommodating narrative tells a positive component of the historical context to emphasize a hopeful outlook for the future.

Public spaces are rigorously gridded in response to the urban fabric toward the National Mall, while the landscape becomes fluid and organic as it faces the riverbank.

Mingxi Li

A Floating Monolith

The transatlantic slave trade meant abduction, abuse, rape, genocide, separation, and alienation that developed into the systemic racism the Black community experiences today. How we address this topic determines how we view history and educate future generations. The history of slavery was not simply a singular narrative repeated on a mass scale but a diverse series of narratives that reveal the suffering, torture, sorrow, strength, resilience, and companionship of countless individuals. Hence the memorial should not manifest only as a singular sculptural element but as a meandering experience in the landscape taking viewers through various stages of history.

One enters the site and descends along a massive triangular pool tilting down toward a dark underpass with gushing water that expresses the agony and sense of loss entailed in the transatlantic slave trade's Middle Passage. In the next part of the journey one turns around and immediately enters a field of triangular pillars, not knowing what lies ahead, with no direction to move but forward. An ascending path guides the visitor toward the final monument—a black monolith with a gradually inclining path—which represents the enduring journey toward recovery and Black power.

Site model, plan view

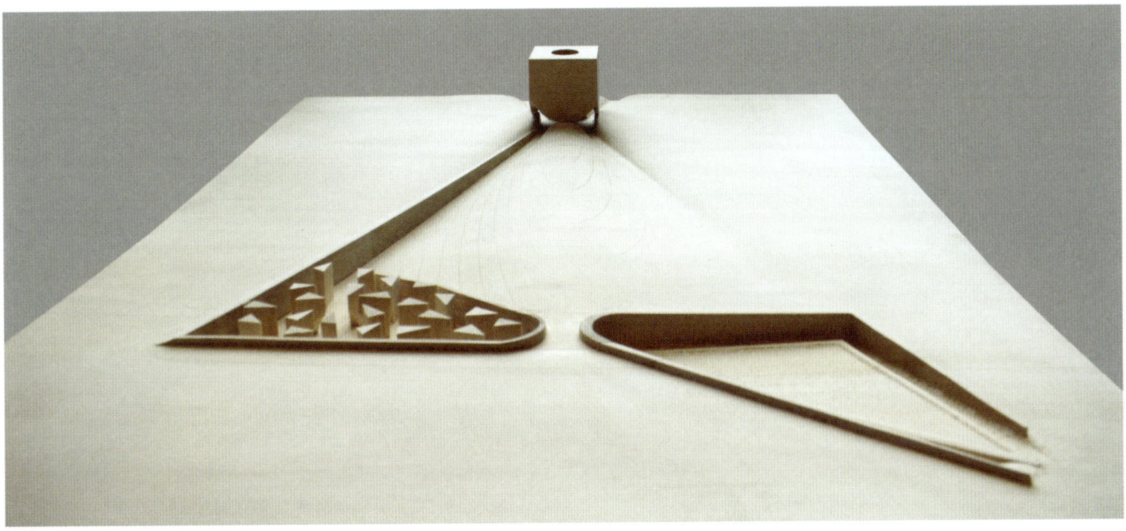

Site model, aerial view looking south

Site model, detail view of black monolith and support mounds

Night view of black monolith in the extended landscape looking south

Rendering of black monolith in the extended landscape looking south (standing between sunken triangular reflecting pool and court)

View toward black monolith from sunken triangular reflecting pool

View under bridge at entry to court of triangular monoliths

View of procession toward entry to the black monolith

Janelle Schmidt

Trace: A Memorial to the Afterlife of Slavery in the United States

Why did slavery happen? Who made the decision? Why Africans? In an attempt to reconcile these questions through architecture, the project spatializes a timeline of slavery, allowing us to see and trace a historical change. While most of Washington, D.C., is subject to how race and discrimination organized land, the studio's memorial site did not exist until 1900. The site terrain was formed of mud dredged from the bottom of the Potomac River, rendering it ahistorical—and allowing an opportunity for the visitors of this memorial to be the first and only ones to mark the land.

The project proposes a memorial program in which an artist leads visitors in a marking ritual that records traces of their presence on the site. Entering the site along a map of old Potomac River topography, visitors pass through an ecological transition—beginning in a forest until they find a clearing. There the artist guides them to collect water from the Potomac, educating them with oral histories along the way. The marking ritual has begun: The artist leads a line of visitors back and forth until their collective footsteps have scored a mark on the ground. The mark then acts as a mold, and the group casts concrete into the mold to make a "trace."

Traces aggregate over time, with generations adding to their family line. In contrast to the Mall's Beaux Arts axes, formed on the backs of the enslaved, this memorial site is organized by ecological boundaries. If future sea levels rise, the marsh at the end of the clearing is free to simply expand, returning to its roots before humans took hold.

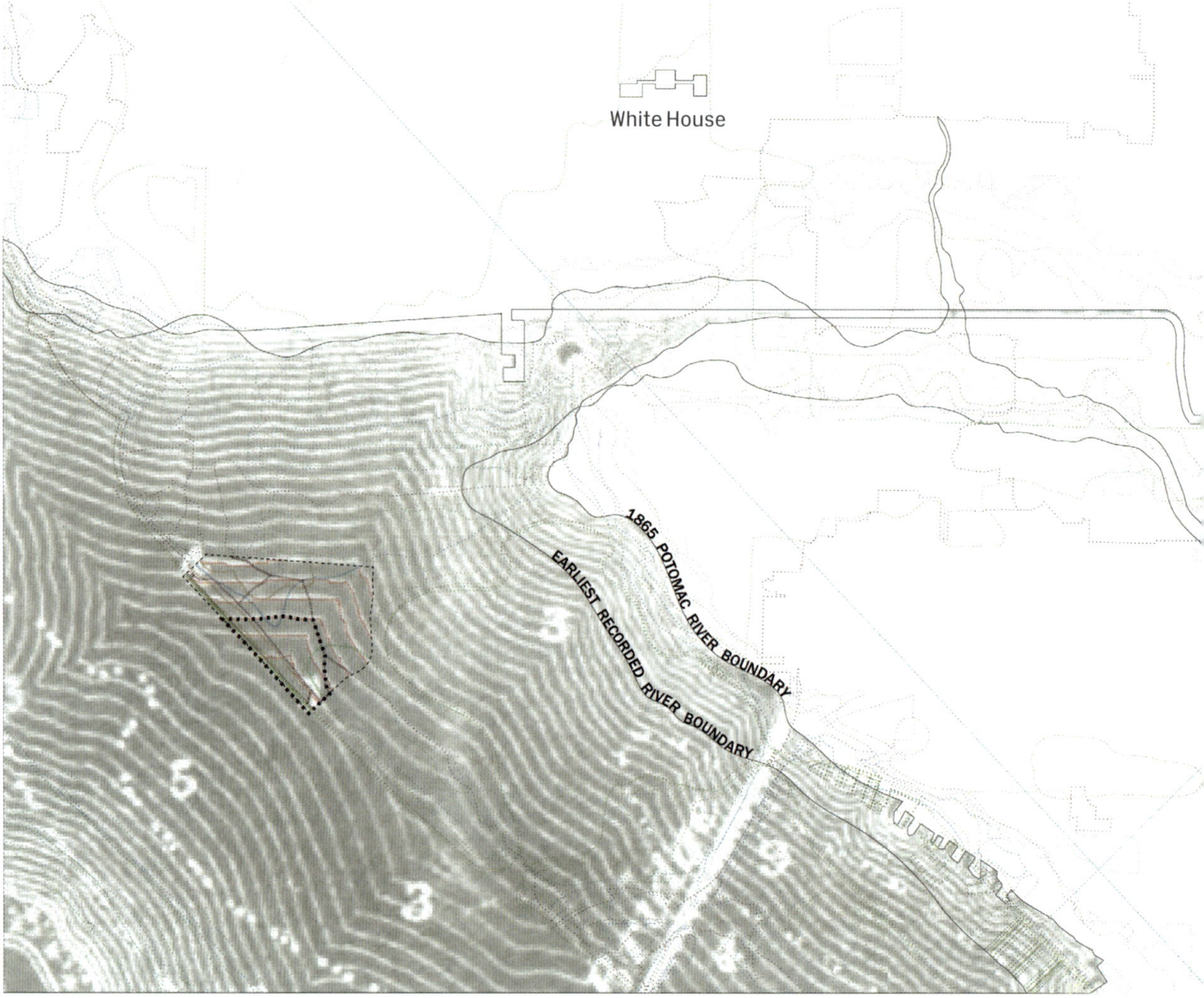

Design analysis between midterm and final review: site map layering the migration of the Potomac River boundary over time, the ecological boundaries on the site, the memorial's site location, and the current location of the White House and the Capitol

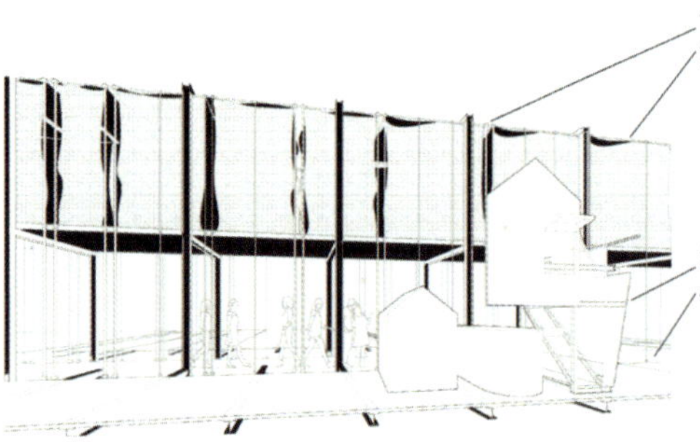

Midterm design: view of "Consequences of Emancipation" screen building. (1) View frame; (2) Emancipation screen building; (3) Interstitial/ quotidian space; (4) Theater set

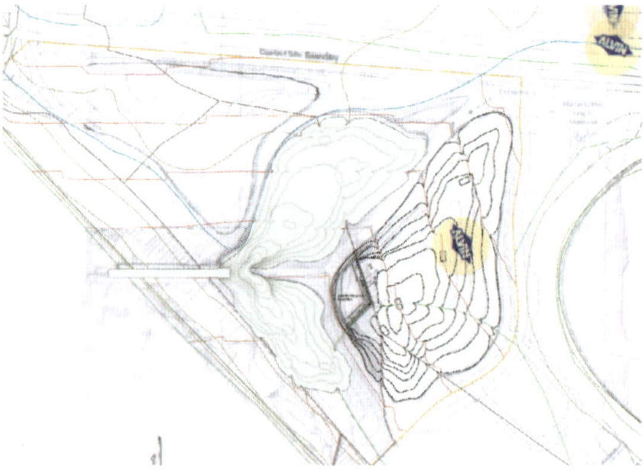

Design progress between midterm and final review: proposed site plan

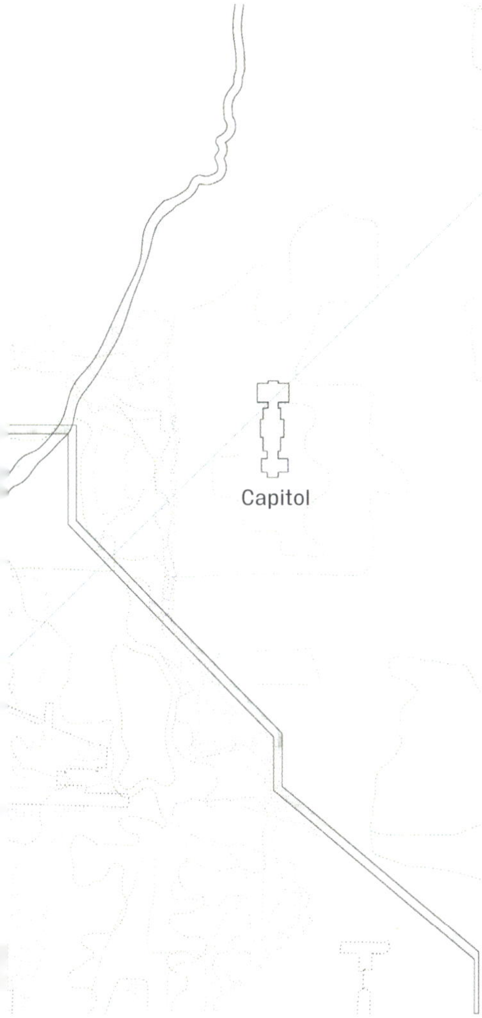

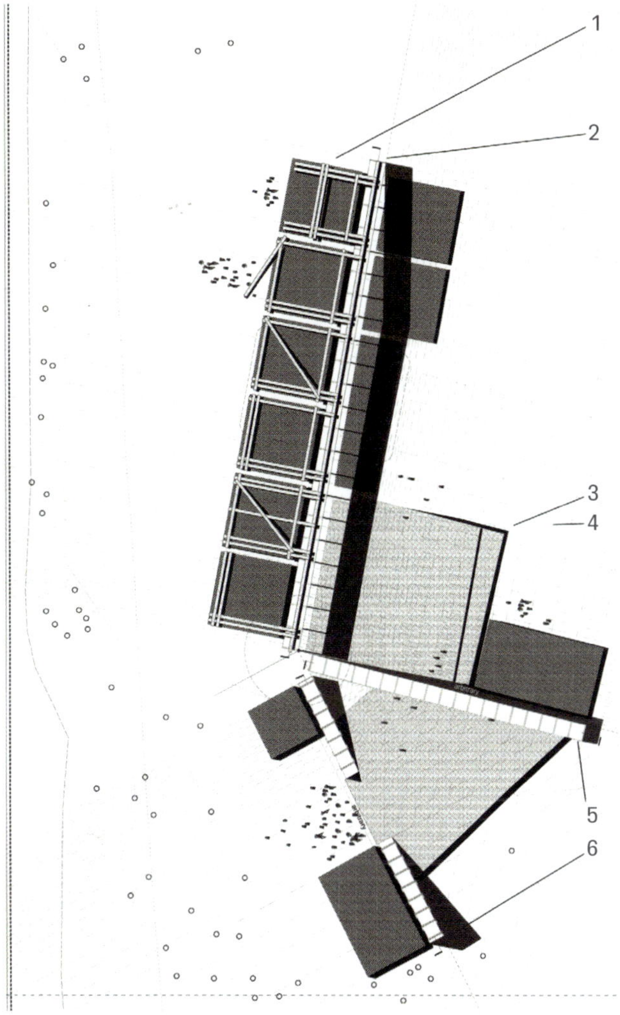

Midterm design: site plan. (1) Theater stage with gantry above; (2) Screen building: "Consequences of Emancipation"; (3) Public space/theater stage; (4) Framed view lines/implied walking routes; (5) Screen building: "Founding of the United States" history; (6) Screen building: "Society, Identity, and Consent" history

Final design: a plaster-cast "trace" of footsteps in the sand

Final design: sectional model of memorial building where the artist's studio is housed

Final design: view of a sacred garden. If visitors follow a path through the forest along an ecological boundary, they will arrive at a sacred garden, where they are free to plant seeds with the help of an artist.

Final design: proposed site plan with the ecological boundaries labeled

Final design: view of the clearing that has three types of impressionable ground (clay, sand [not pictured], and exposed soil) in which visitors can make a "trace"

Final design: 1/128" = 1'- 0" site model showing the forest, the building, and the different types of ground on the site

Final design: proposed 3D site plan and 2D floor plans

Abeer Seikaly, Weaving a Home, Tent at Al-Namara near the Dead Sea, Jordan, 2020

ABEER SEIKALY

Conscious Skins

INTERVIEW

First published in Yale's *Constructs*

Nina Rappaport
How did you decide, as a young Jordanian-Palestinian woman in 1997, to go to RISD to study design and architecture, and how did that step determine your future?

Abeer Seikaly
I learned about RISD through my art teacher, Samia Zaru. I liked that it was a small school focused on art and offered an opportunity to navigate through different disciplines. In my home environment my mother and grandmother opened up different ways of seeing. However, my first year at RISD was extremely challenging, and it humbled me. Then it slowly built me back up again, and it was one of the most transformative experiences of my life. It was a foundational journey for what I do today—how I work, the way I think, and where I am.

One of your early studies focuses on weaving, an Indigenous craft that engages both materiality and form throughout history. It also echoes Gottfried Semper's theories of *Verkleidung*, or woven walls, and is now even being engaged in new digital technologies by architects. How have you incorporated Arab weaving traditions as structure into your contemporary "high-tech" project Weaving a Home?

I've been questioning this idea of low-tech versus high-tech. When we look at traditional work, we compare it to today's technology, but if you look at the root meaning of the word *technology*, it is art and making. The weaving of a basket 100 years ago was done in the technology of the times. Weaving makes crucial use, as an act, as a process, of your body and mind in a relationship that is the foundation of Indigenous social practices and knowledge. What has changed are the tools enabling us to create new forms and meanings that reflect our needs and how we live today.

Abeer Seikaly, Weaving a Home, Tent at Al-Namara near the Dead Sea, Jordan, 2020

How have you focused on materials and your relationship to eye, hand, and object?

I am a tactile person and have always worked with model making, so my process is led very much by craft. That being said, this intersection between tradition and contemporary technology is reflected in what I do and how I work. The materials I work with channel different forms of making. I am also looking at unfolding in origami and kirigami and how we combine fabric and structure so they become one. It is like synthesizing traditional practices with models, systems, and structures that are adaptable and can perform different tasks. The meeting point between new and old is rooted in both the way I work and my personal background. My mom comes from a very traditional background and my dad from a very contemporary family, so the merging of those worlds has always interested me.

How does your fascination with mathematical systems and geometrical patterns reflect your use of structure and form in textiles? Parts of your dome-tent project remind me of Chuck Hoberman's expandable structural systems, yet his are rigid while yours are soft and woven.

My musical background has influenced my interest in clear structure and rhythm reflected in physical form. I see a whole but also the pieces that come together to make that whole. I am also interested in movement, flexibility, and transformation.

Abeer Seikaly, Meeting Points, detail from exhibition *La Manufacture*, Lille Métropole, World Design Capital, photograph by Paul Tahon, 2020

Weaving is a way of thinking that has allowed me to express different geometries. I like sequences, repetition, and patterns, but I don't draw lines; my process always begins with a model. Model making has allowed me to understand objects, forms, and spaces in a three-dimensional way. I am very intrigued by notions of sacred geometry and how they manifest in different forms as metaphor.

How did you conceptualize your project Weaving a Home, based on your studio project at RISD? What was the process of turning it into a deployable structure with all of the necessities of home, and how did the project change over time?

At RISD I was interested in creating fabric architecture. We think about fabric and structure as being things that are disengaged, so I investigated how we can combine them into one. My project is rooted in this technical exploration. From a metaphorical point of view, I have been interested in the notion of home and shelter, of the womb and the mother, since day one. During spring term 2001, I took an advanced studio that was offered as part of a design competition, which asked us to examine and invent fabric architecture for the use of a disaster-relief shelter. I left that project alone for many years until I entered the competition for the international Lexus Design Award. The theme of movement resonated with me, so I linked the system I created at RISD with a meaningful crisis—the Syrian refugee crisis and the 60 million displaced people around the world—to provide a dignified shelter. I used the folding fabric I had designed at RISD for a tent, and it received an award. My intention was to weave a displaced community together as a home.

At this point you've made the prototypes, but have you found a place where they can actually be deployed by any of the agencies?

For about four years I worked on developing the structure with the engineering firm Atelier One. Through the process of constructing the tent, I gained a deep insight into materials, processes, and the importance of collaborating with various communities to understand different social contexts and environments using local building technologies. I became more and more skeptical with imposing shelter on a community. I went to a Zaatari camp and spoke to a lot of NGOs, and I became discouraged about how the humanitarian organizations work with refugees.

How did you shift your direction and change the tent concept?

My research on Bedouin tent-making two years ago was a turning point. I decided that rather than make the project within a refugee context I would research cultural heritage on a deeper level to develop new processes for building a home. I began to work with communities to learn how to build using local materials and help people fabricate dignified shelters. Questions surfaced, such as: How can the design of a shelter create added value? How can architecture become a social technology and a cultural practice? But the main question that allowed me to answer all of these is a very simple one: What is the material of the tent made from? I didn't know at first, but now I can safely say I am interested in wool, in goat hair—a local building material that is also environmentally friendly.

When you talk about the idea of home are you more interested in a permanent structure or a Bedouin-style nomadic shelter? Are you considering how we build in cities or only how local nomads move from place to place?

This is a very good question, and two years ago I would have had a totally different answer before I worked on a film that juxtaposed the handmade home created by women versus men building with concrete. I now see a marriage between the Bedouin tent, the textile, and the concrete. Sometimes Bedouins are forced to move into villages and live in more permanent houses, but they're still attached to their roots and way of living in something that is flexible and movable. They might have a concrete block wall in the courtyard, but the roof is a tent. I too am interested in more flexible structures.

A project that I think continues your interest in connections to and with the community is Meeting Points. How was it both a tactile and physical project as well as a collaboration on a specific site?

When I started working on Bedouin tent-making craftsmanship and understanding the wool and goat hair used in making those homes, I made it my mission to develop a system using those materials. It is not the tent that is innovative in Weaving a Home; it is the material system that could become a tent or a canopy. Meeting Points was the process of creating a material system like the tent. The tapestry is inherently experimental. It does not provide a solution to a problem but rather poses questions on how and why it could be used in terms of its limitations and potentials. It's a structure that cherishes the symbiotic nature of our cultural heritage expressed through the gentle act of weaving, which brings together different elements to create a new cultural form.

Who worked on the project, and how did you get them involved?

Meeting Points was a collaboration between 58 members of Bedouin and rural communities, including 40 women, from various areas across Jordan. I would meet one person and go to an event, and the interest just spread as I got to know them. We began with clipping the goat hair, spinning the yarn, knitting, and putting the structure together. It showed that it is not what we design and build but how we choose to design and build with different people. My process is very methodical, and with women it's always a two-way relationship formed through conversation around what we are doing and building as well as who we are, what we do, how we live, and so on. I learn from them as much as they learn from me.

How did this project relate to your overall interest in home?

It continued my personal and collective mission to really understand what home is, what it means to dwell in the twenty-first century. It doesn't have to be a static answer; it's always evolving and can mean different things for different people, but that's what drives everything I do.

Were you okay during the pandemic we are just emerging from?

Oh my, there was a period when it didn't really matter whether I worked or did not work. But then both I and my parents were affected by the virus, and I spent about two and a half months doing nothing other than taking care of them. During that period I moved my studio to another location.

I'm sorry you and your family had the coronavirus but glad to hear you could work. Teaching kept many people going, although it was difficult online. Why do you teach, and what is your Yale studio site and topic?

It is going to be very interesting to teach within the walls of an institution. I've always been rebellious and promoted new ways of teaching beyond university boundaries. Teaching provides me the opportunity to try to understand not only that way of thinking but also my process and how I'm communicating it to the students. I love teaching as a conversation that you form with students, each of whom has a unique way of looking at things.

ESSAY

Weaving as a Cultural Microcosm: Rediscovering Tradition in Modern Architecture

At the heart of Bedouin weaving lies the ground loom, an essential tool used by nomadic women in the Middle East and North Africa to weave textiles. This simple and portable apparatus, set directly on the ground, consists of warp threads stretched between two parallel poles held apart by pegs. Weft threads interlace over and under the warp threads to create the finished textile. Beyond its utilitarian purpose, the ground loom serves as the nucleus of communal interaction and homemaking in Bedouin tribes. It is central to their daily lives, enabling them to create and dismantle woven textile cloths for their homes as they traverse the desert.

The act of weaving transcends mere craftsmanship; it is inherently a communal process. Bedouin communities come together to create their tents, and this sense of collaboration and shared tradition extends to the entire community. Weaving is not just a solitary act but a collective effort involving multiple generations. The young learn from the old, and each member plays a role in creating a shelter that is vital for their way of life. In an era marked increasingly by industrialization and urbanization, the traditional nomadic culture of the Arab world has been fading into the archives of history.

What lessons can we learn from traditional weaving practices and the principles it represents? How can contemporary architecture evolve to become more flexible in the way Bedouin tents adjust to the desert's demands?

Weaving as Social Architecture for Sustainable Urban Landscapes

The revival of weaving traditions offers a significant shift in perspective on architecture, sustainability, culture, and human interconnectedness. In the face of rampant industrialization and urbanization, there is a growing need to rethink our approach to architecture and urban development. Weaving can comprise a guiding philosophy that reshapes our interactions with time and space and inspires cradle-to-cradle architecture that promotes environmental and social benefits.

The essence of weaving as a modus operandi goes beyond the physical act of creating textiles; it includes weaving together values and principles that can guide our modern society. One key principle is adaptability. Bedouin culture, with its deep connection to weaving, has thrived in arid and transient environments. The ground loom represents a form of knowledge that embraces scarcity and turns it into an opportunity for resourcefulness. This approach is a stark contrast to prevailing architectural practices that rely on sedentary, environmentally damaging materials. Emphasizing principles of adaptability and resourcefulness in architecture can lead to structures that can evolve and adapt, just as Bedouin tents do as they traverse the desert.

Cradle-to-cradle architecture, a concept that emphasizes the sustainable life cycles of materials and buildings, can benefit greatly from weaving as a model. Traditional weaving is inherently sustainable; it starts with raw materials, involves human skill and craftsmanship, and results in functional and beautiful textiles. These textiles can be reused and repurposed, and they eventually return to the earth without causing harm. This circular approach to materials and production aligns perfectly with the principles of sustainability and environmental responsibility.

Weaving also connects us to our cultural traditions. In a rapidly changing world where globalization is homogenizing cultures, preserving and celebrating diversity is essential. The act of weaving, passed down through generations, carries with it the wisdom, stories, and traditions of the past. It reminds us of the importance of honoring our cultural heritage while embracing innovation.

Conscious Skins: Reintegrating Cultural Heritage into Modern Modes of Production

These principles were integral to my approach and methodology for the advanced design studio "Conscious Skins." The students began their investigations by identifying a specific Indigenous craft tradition focused around an existing fabric structure, textile technique, and in some cases, a related material ecology. The first half of the semester was spent pursuing this textile knowledge, exploring materials, and replicating, translating, and transforming practices of hand-making. Documentation of their investigations and creative processes was a key requirement. By documenting their work, the students were able to articulate and reflect on their thought processes, design decisions, and material choices. Documentation also allowed for a deeper exploration of the cultural and social contexts surrounding the craft traditions being explored, providing a platform for critical engagement and dialogue.

The intersection of the students' rigorous experimentation with materials and their interaction with the larger cosmology of hand-making culminated in the design of a comprehensive system for textile production. This process deepened their comprehension of the spatial and conceptual complexity of creating "devices," "structural fabrics," and "soft architectures." It also led them to a heightened awareness of a different conception of time and a more thoughtful approach to the process of making.

The emphasis on textiles in my work—and in this design studio—has always stemmed from my admiration for the Bedouin tent, known in Arabic as *Beit al Sha'ar*, meaning "house of hair." The word *tent* is derived from the Latin *tendere*, meaning "to stretch." Woven from goat's hair and sheep's wool, the Bedouin tent has the ability to contract and expand, making it adaptable to changes in the weather. Wool is versatile due to its excellent tensile properties, allowing it to be stretched and molded into various ways.

Crafting a New Narrative for Time and Space

As an architect I am inspired by the tent's capacity to adapt and transform with the environment, reflecting the way the loom turns fibers into woven fabrics. This quality enables me to push the boundaries of textile design, exploring new techniques and materials to create structures that are not only aesthetically pleasing but also functionally innovative. By stretching and manipulating the materials, I create new geometric potentials, transforming two-dimensional planes into three-dimensional forms that have a stronger connection to surrounding space.

Embracing weaving as a model holds the potential to reshape our relationship with time and space. Championing communal and collective building processes can pave the way for cradle-to-cradle architecture, ushering in environmental and social benefits for our urban landscapes. Weaving, with its deep roots in tradition and its inherent adaptability, challenges the linear trajectory of architectural evolution by advocating for a circular approach rooted in the present yet enriched by the wisdom of the past.

STUDIO BRIEF

Conscious Skins

Merging Traditional Craft Practices and Twenty-First-Century Architectonics

Our daily lives are threatened by intertwined crises: wars, climate change, and global pandemics have stretched economic and health systems to their breaking points. The spatial problems within our communities are caused largely by the rigid structures of the built urban environment. In contrast, traditional building practices emphasize a conscious, responsive, and nimble relationship with the environment as a foundational principle. Contemporary architecture needs to adapt and respond to local contexts and needs. Through experimentation with traditional materials, technologies, and forms, there is potential to create spaces that sustain the human spirit and the natural environment.

A dynamic alternative to the rigid, heavy building model of modern Western architecture is fabric construction. This deeply rooted cultural and social practice results in soft, flexible shelters. From the *Beit al Sha'ar,* a Bedouin tent made of goat's hair, to the Mongolian yurt, traditional fabric structures are constructed with locally available tools—the most pertinent the craftsperson's own body. For the *Beit al Sha'ar,* a woman uses her skilled hands and intuition to stretch and weave the material and her body as a measuring device to gauge scale and size. The structure is infused with elements of its environment, from the raw material extracted from indigenous animals to the tools used in the building process.

The studio began with the definition of weaving as a technology rooted in the hand—celebrating the hand as technology and craft as innovation. The work created in the studio took shape through experimentation with different material systems, not as derivatives of a building mechanism but as generative drivers within the design process. The central vision aimed to reposition the process as a central aspect of building. As such, the studio challenged the narrow perception of architecture as a static artifact or "matter," instead treating it as a dynamic, living process.

Textile Traditions and Cultural Narratives

"Conscious Skins" prompted students to approach textile making as a spatial, social, and affective engagement with materials and context. They began their investigations by identifying a specific Indigenous craft tradition focused around a fabric structure, textile techniques, and in some cases, a related material ecology. Each tradition served as a portal into the cultural and historical landscape from which it emerged. These crafts are more than just fabrications; they are repositories of knowledge, tales of civilizations, and embodiments of cultural identity. Through the studio students slowly began to decode the hidden narratives embedded within fabrics.

The students spent the first half of the semester pursuing this textile knowledge, exploring materials, and replicating, translating, and transforming handmade practices. They explored the physical attributes of textile artifacts as well as their broader sociocultural implications. One of the main requirements of the studio was the documentation of the students' investigations and work process. The evolution of the studio saw students grappling with the intersection of tradition and innovation.

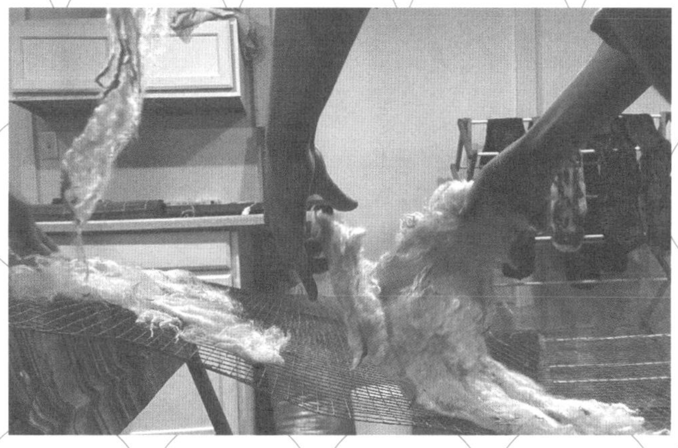

This phase introduced another layer of complexity to their explorations and spawned the following questions: How did materials and processes mirror the environments and communities from which they originated? What silent narratives did these textiles convey? How could age-old techniques find relevance in the modern world? What novel possibilities might emerge from this fusion of past and present?

Stretching the Studio Brief

Architecture and textiles share major concerns in terms of goals but have little in common in terms of language, materials, processes, and technologies. During travel week to Upstate New York we visited textile labs and studios of practitioners whose modes of production emerge from collective thinking rather than centralized systems relying on extraction and competition. This experience offered students the opportunity to enter into an ecosystem of fiber agriculture, namely sheep's wool, to see firsthand where the materials originate and how both manual and industrialized processes (washing, carding, spinning, felting, dyeing, weaving) contribute to fabric structures. Insight into the holistic cycle and spatial interplay within which fiber processing occurs inspired ideas as to how their textile creations and the respective contexts of fabrication could organically give rise to programs reliant on the material vocabularies they developed.

The students' rigorous material experimentation intersected with their engagement in the larger cosmology of hand-making. The process offered them a deeper understanding of the spatial aspects inherent in the act of making that guided them in crafting an entire system of production. This understanding was instrumental in the development of both physical and conceptual elements, including "devices," "structural fabrics," and "soft architectures." It is with this visceral feeling that reaches out to their "skin"—through touch—that their processes of "making" became more "conscious" experiences of time (or "time experience") and more intentional approaches toward thinking through textiles.

Outcome: The Studio as a Framework for Exploration

The outcome of the studio is a process. The documentation of the work unfolding through various forms of media served as a frame and ground for questions, experiments, and subjective reflections on making. Each exercise was guided by a question that served as a method, instrument, technique, and practice strengthening the students' thought processes and how they are communicated. This self-conscious approach defined the fundamental premise and primary inquiries that the studio explored: How can we rethink the role of crafts in the context of contemporary building practices in the digital age? How can traditional knowledge systems and material cultures contribute to the development of new material technologies? How can alternative methods of using traditional materials (or creating new types of materials) cultivate a more sensitive relationship to long-standing cultural practices and to the environment?

Thinking through Textile Making

The diverse origin points, intentions, and idiosyncrasies of the student's creative processes brought equally assorted results. The students all extended their focused, small-scale work of hand-making to a bigger, more complex spatial proposition. Their reproductions of Indigenous textile practices were made within both the personal spaces of their homes ("first space") and the social space of the studio ("second space"). They learned from one another's approaches to making and drew inspiration from experts who shared their research and work on structural material systems and fabrication. They connected with places and people and reflected on their own process through textile construction.

The Intimacy of Objects and Spaces

As Karl Marx remarked, in the capitalist mode of production labor does not produce just commodities but also "the worker as a commodity." Industrial production has alienated us from our sensory relationship with material and making, numbing our sense of being and becoming. The intimacy of creating objects and the labors involved in producing them (through a variety of tools and mediums) combats this loss of identity. In this studio each student was in charge of the whole process of design, placed at the center of creation, recording every movement, thought, and experiment.

Tradition is still alive while it happens. In tradition there are possibilities for change—reformation of preexisting materials and processes. We encouraged the students to think about the work generated in the studio as a collective research project and to identify how their personal explorations intersected with other projects. Before the final stretch of the studio we asked them to consider the following questions: How does the new structural skin accommodate the body and shelter the process of its own manufacture? What new relations—between maker and user, body and architecture, X and Y—does your project make possible?

For the final review students were asked to communicate their positions as "conscious" makers; to discuss the physical and conceptual frameworks and/or objects of their constructions; and to relate the "textile idea" of their projects and the sociotechnical assemblage involved in fabricating the three-dimensional textiles. Navigating through distinct spatiotemporal patterns of expression (through "first and second spaces"), we see the final review as a "third space"—an experience that facilitates a broader and more creative form of interaction. Since weaving is a dialogue between loom and weaver, its ritual of repetitive motion opens the weaver to the inner dialogue directing actions and allowing for the possibility of change. So a mindful moment in time is captured in the cloth created. From tradition to innovation, the studio proved that textiles are still new frontiers for us all to explore. How has this wealth of process—directed with intention from the mind to the hand and into each final work—crossed between chaos and order, construction and deconstruction, strength and fragility? The students demonstrated this diversity in their processes and presented the entire spatiality of the system of production in their textiles.

Transcending the boundaries of conventional design pedagogy, the "Conscious Skins" studio was a transformative exploration of textile traditions and material culture as a way to enrich architectural and spatial design and thinking. It challenged students to view textiles not as passive materials but as active agents in the dialogue between tradition and modernity, material and space, structure and fabric. From this experience they will carry forward a heightened consciousness of textiles and their potential to shape the built environment.

The studio emphasized the intimate connections between creative processes and the contexts in which they unfold. Much like a spider at the center of its web, students recognized that responses to context are grounded inherently in the bodily experiences of individuals situated in a particular space, time, and culture. This web of relations places the maker at the core, perceiving and interpreting the world subjectively while remaining entwined within it. The studio will live on through the tactile productions, thoughtful reflections, and enduring questions that emerged along the way.

STUDENT WORK

Adare Brown

Stav Dror

Serge Saab

Elise Limon

Hao Tang

Jun Nam

Morgan Kerber

Sydney Maubert

Smaranda Rusinaru

Taiga Taba

Adare Brown

Reed Source

Phragmites (Phragmites australis) is an invasive monoculture dominating the Quinnipiac Tidal Marsh and acting as an effective mediator of the heavy metals plaguing the formerly industrial Quinnipiac River. However the tidal wetland remains alienated and isolated from the surrounding city since the only public point of access is an overlook trail accessible from the parking lot behind Target and Buffalo Wild Wings, in the North Haven Pavilion shopping center. The land is owned by the state of Connecticut, and despite advocacy efforts spearheaded by the Quinnipiac River Watershed Partnership and the New Haven Bird Club, no substantive restoration plans have been put in place by the state since 2004.

Given the stalemate at the state level, this project engages directly with the marsh to imagine opportunities for public programs beyond recreation and observation. Thus, rather than accept Phragmites as invaders, I considered it as a material source for casting paper. At the site I cut and harvested Phragmites, using rice cookers, deep fryers, bread makers, and blenders purchased from an adjacent Goodwill Outlet to render the reeds into viable paper pulp. Cued into the culture of papermaking by Lillian Bellís's book *Plant Fibers for Papermaking*, I produced a Phragmites recipe book—a common form of knowledge sharing in the papermaking community. The result of the project is a matrix of sheets in 80 varieties indexed to the recipe book, demonstrating the material capacity of this reed source to yield divergent forms and images.

Excerpts of drawing, writing, and photography recorded in the process book

15

Building footprints in the New Haven metro area. Bound by industry on either side, the marsh has little presence in the city despite its impressive size.

Topographic map of New Haven: the marsh and the snaking Quinnipiac River

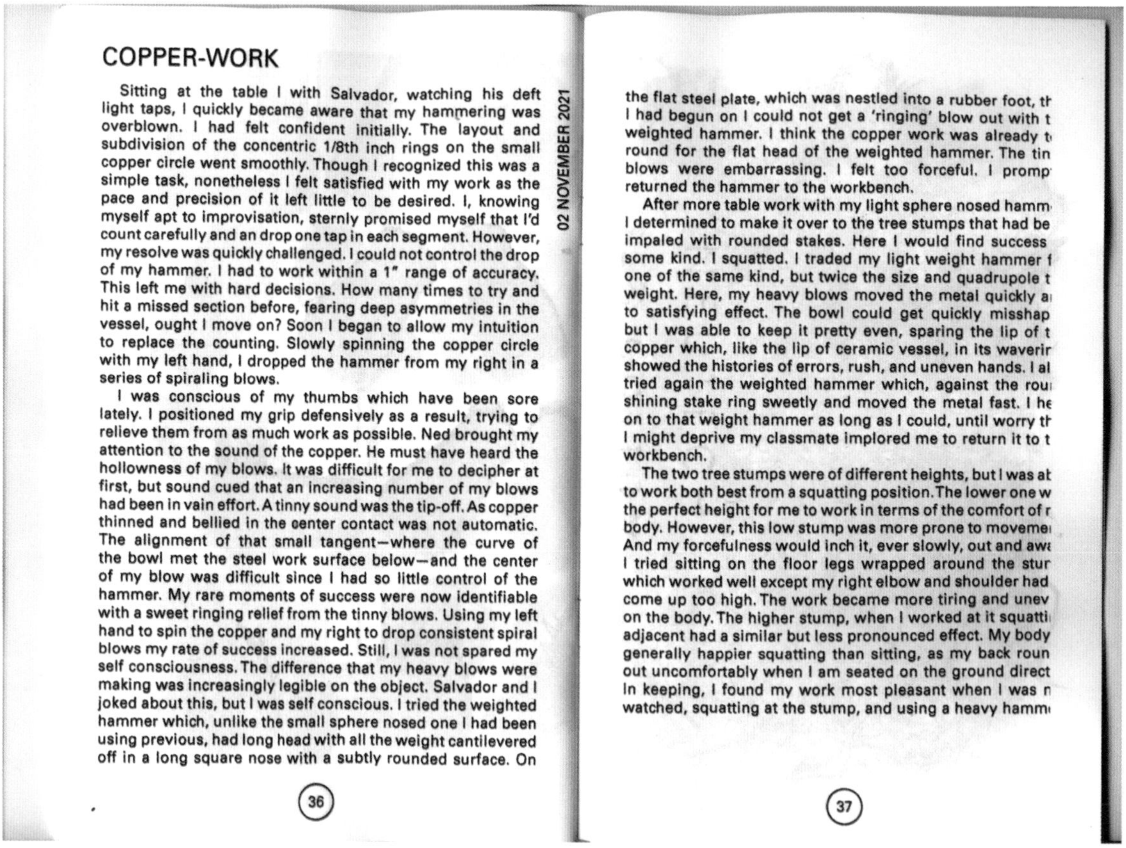

COPPER-WORK

02 NOVEMBER 2021

Sitting at the table I with Salvador, watching his deft light taps, I quickly became aware that my hammering was overblown. I had felt confident initially. The layout and subdivision of the concentric 1/8th inch rings on the small copper circle went smoothly. Though I recognized this was a simple task, nonetheless I felt satisfied with my work as the pace and precision of it left little to be desired. I, knowing myself apt to improvisation, sternly promised myself that I'd count carefully and an drop one tap in each segment. However, my resolve was quickly challenged. I could not control the drop of my hammer. I had to work within a 1" range of accuracy. This left me with hard decisions. How many times to try and hit a missed section before, fearing deep asymmetries in the vessel, ought I move on? Soon I began to allow my intuition to replace the counting. Slowly spinning the copper circle with my left hand, I dropped the hammer from my right in a series of spiraling blows.

I was conscious of my thumbs which have been sore lately. I positioned my grip defensively as a result, trying to relieve them from as much work as possible. Ned brought my attention to the sound of the copper. He must have heard the hollowness of my blows. It was difficult for me to decipher at first, but sound cued that an increasing number of my blows had been in vain effort. A tinny sound was the tip-off. As copper thinned and bellied in the center contact was not automatic. The alignment of that small tangent—where the curve of the bowl met the steel work surface below—and the center of my blow was difficult since I had so little control of the hammer. My rare moments of success were now identifiable with a sweet ringing relief from the tinny blows. Using my left hand to spin the copper and my right to drop consistent spiral blows my rate of success increased. Still, I was not spared my self consciousness. The difference that my heavy blows were making was increasingly legible on the object. Salvador and I joked about this, but I was self conscious. I tried the weighted hammer which, unlike the small sphere nosed one I had been using previous, had long head with all the weight cantilevered off in a long square nose with a subtly rounded surface. On

36

the flat steel plate, which was nestled into a rubber foot, th
I had begun on I could not get a 'ringing' blow out with t
weighted hammer. I think the copper work was already t
round for the flat head of the weighted hammer. The tin
blows were embarrassing. I felt too forceful. I promp
returned the hammer to the workbench.

After more table work with my light sphere nosed hamm
I determined to make it over to the tree stumps that had be
impaled with rounded stakes. Here I would find success
some kind. I squatted. I traded my light weight hammer f
one of the same kind, but twice the size and quadrupole t
weight. Here, my heavy blows moved the metal quickly a
to satisfying effect. The bowl could get quickly misshap
but I was able to keep it pretty even, sparing the lip of t
copper which, like the lip of ceramic vessel, in its waverir
showed the histories of errors, rush, and uneven hands. I al
tried again the weighted hammer which, against the rou
shining stake ring sweetly and moved the metal fast. I he
on to that weight hammer as long as I could, until worry th
I might deprive my classmate implored me to return it to t
workbench.

The two tree stumps were of different heights, but I was ab
to work both best from a squatting position. The lower one w
the perfect height for me to work in terms of the comfort of r
body. However, this low stump was more prone to moveme
And my forcefulness would inch it, ever slowly, out and aw
I tried sitting on the floor legs wrapped around the stur
which worked well except my right elbow and shoulder had
come up too high. The work became more tiring and unev
on the body. The higher stump, when I worked at it squatti
adjacent had a similar but less pronounced effect. My body
generally happier squatting than sitting, as my back roun
out uncomfortably when I am seated on the ground direct
In keeping, I found my work most pleasant when I was n
watched, squatting at the stump, and using a heavy hamm

37

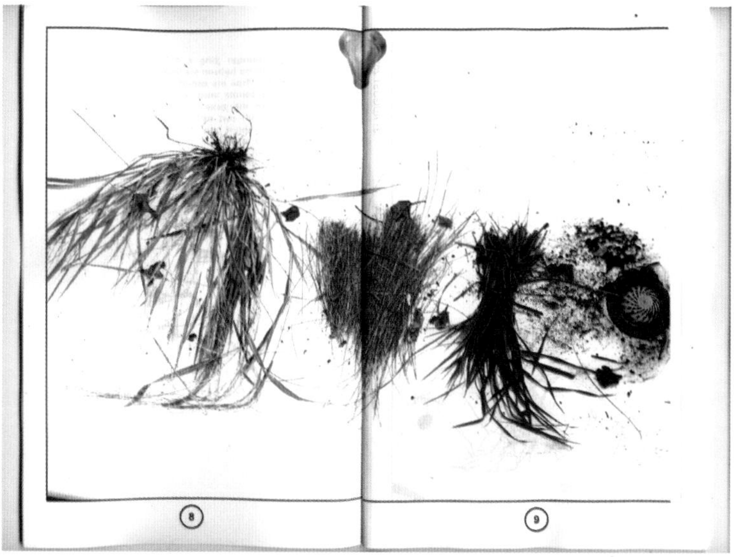

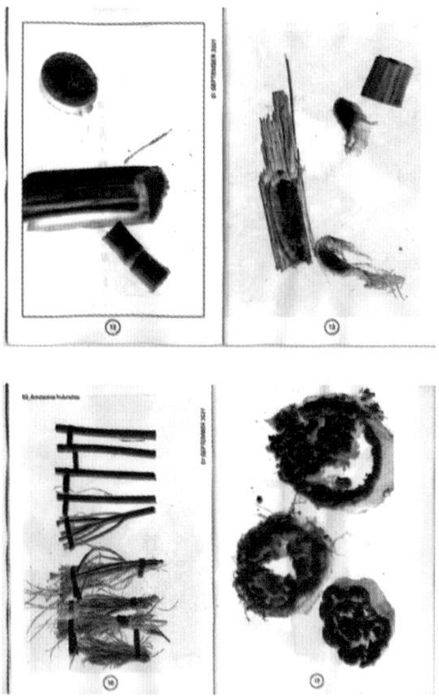

The design project was complemented by a practice of archiving, conversation, and adventure. These are samples of some of the drawings, writings, and photographs recorded in the process book.

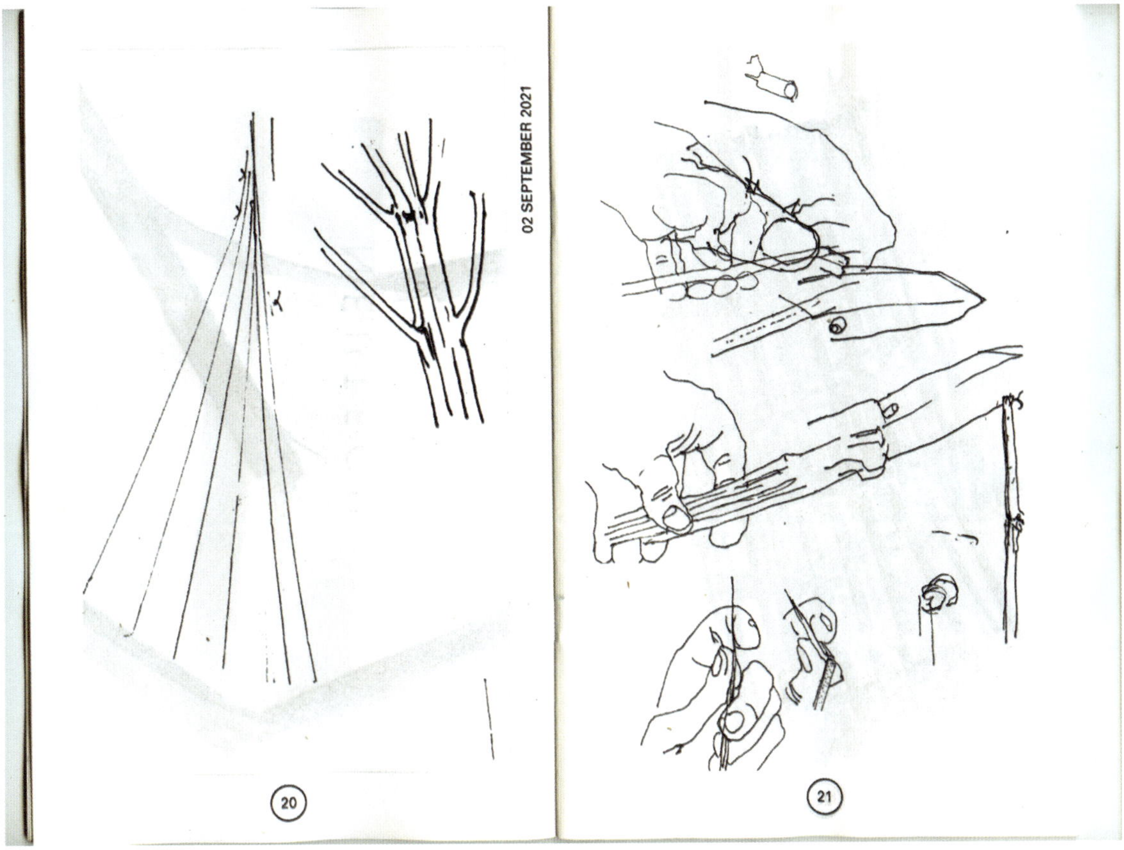

The design project was complemented by a practice of archiving, conversation, and adventure.

The 80 varieties developed to demonstrate the material capacity of the reed source, yielding divergent forms and images.

Stav Dror, Serge Saab, Elise Limon

Very Small, Hardly There

This project investigates the essence of textile making through the development of a system that embraces the inherent textile qualities of slackness and softness to reorganize space and program. The knotted system holds onto and wraps itself, stretches between, and hangs off the site where it exists while transforming its section. The artifact visually obscures its functional elements, making it useless in structural terms but useful in terms of program. The fundamentals of textile making—chords, knots, tools, and the body—are combined to choreograph a set of new situations that emerge from existing ones. The lack of familiar structural qualities—volume, stiffness, stability—is central to the system's capacity to transcend the conventions of space. It is not space, but it is spatial. It is not structure, but it is structuring. Rather than thinking how to stiffen textile into a wall, we take on the existence of the wall itself. What can be extracted from textile to change our understanding and experience of program and space?

Balcony fragment model: Elevation theater

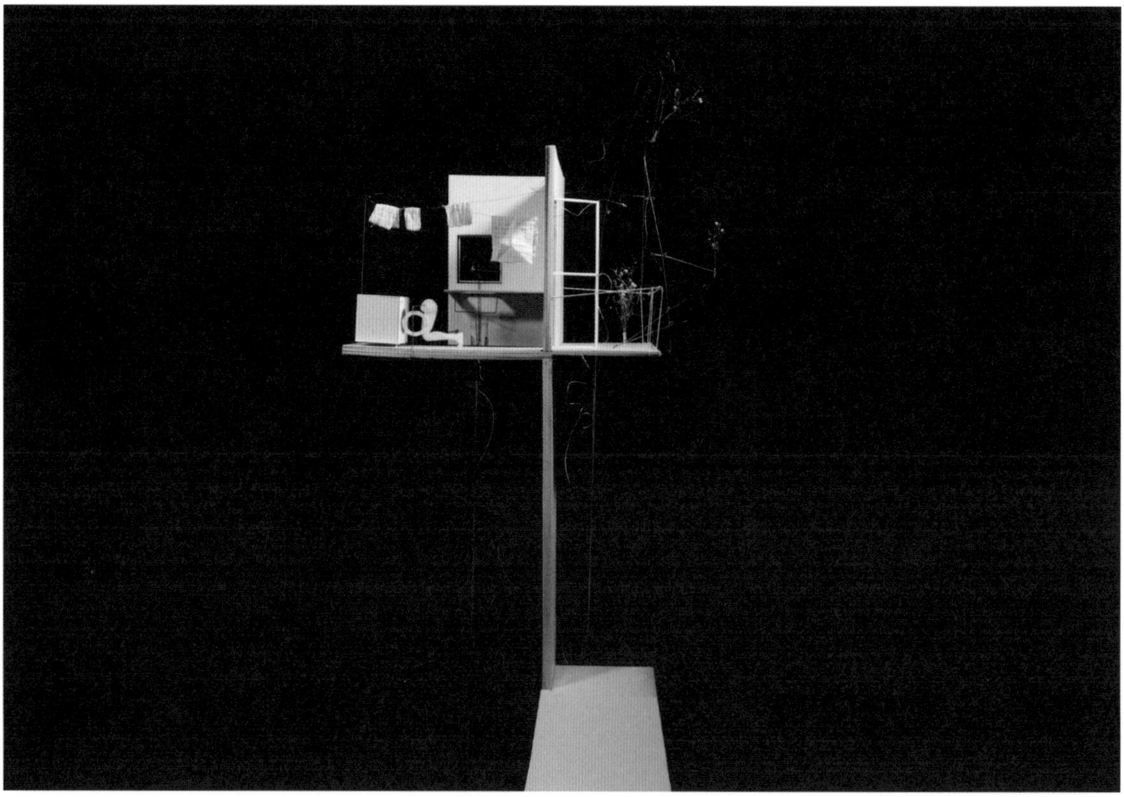

Balcony fragment model: The minimum of what allows the knots to operate

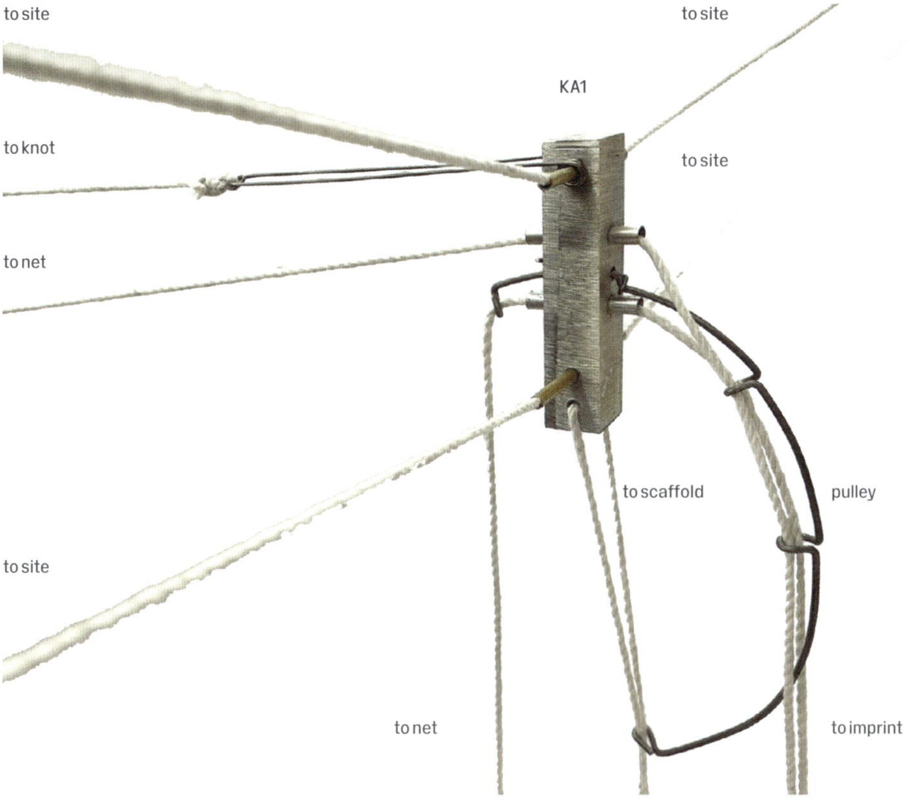

Structural knot: a 1:1 model stretching cords across space, iterating its programs

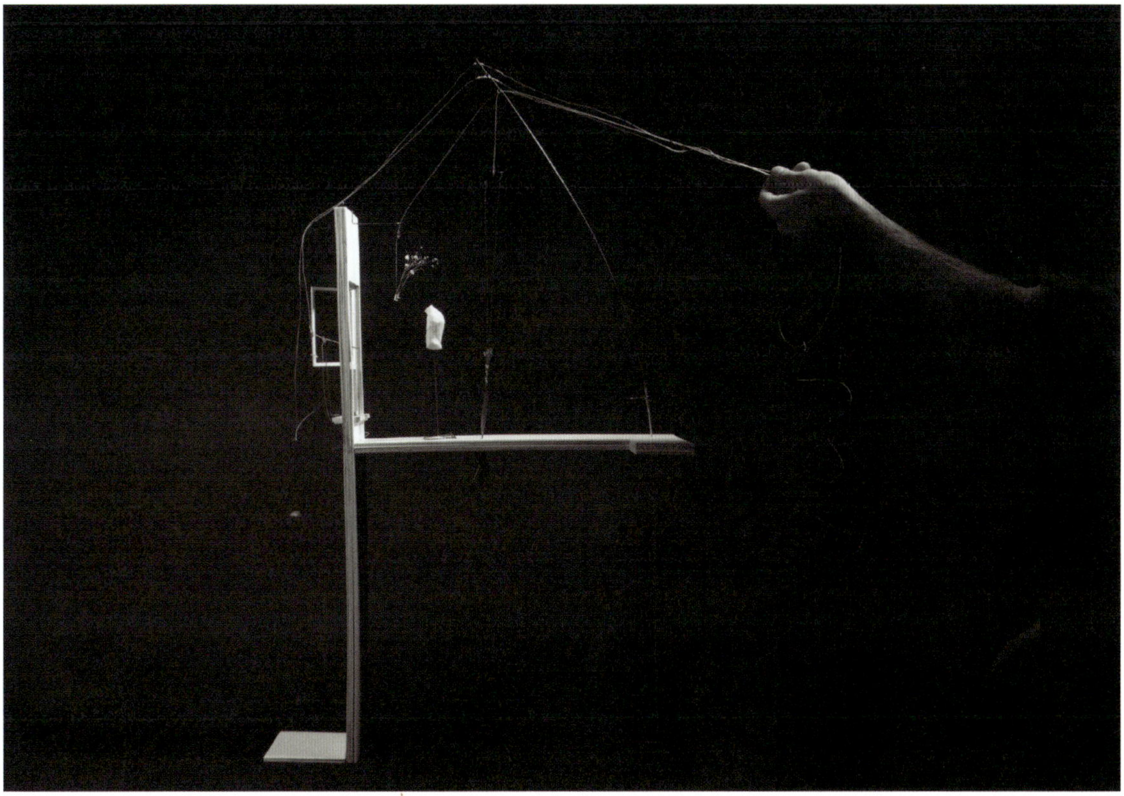

Window fragment model: The interior sequence as it pours out

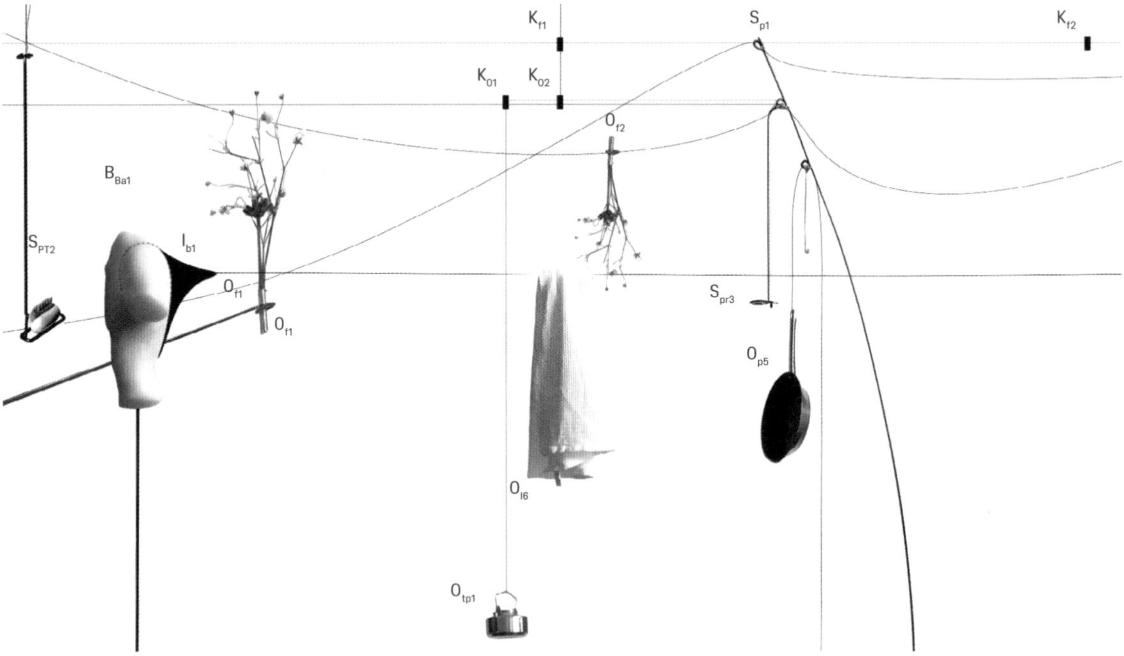

Window: Hotdog sequence section and notation

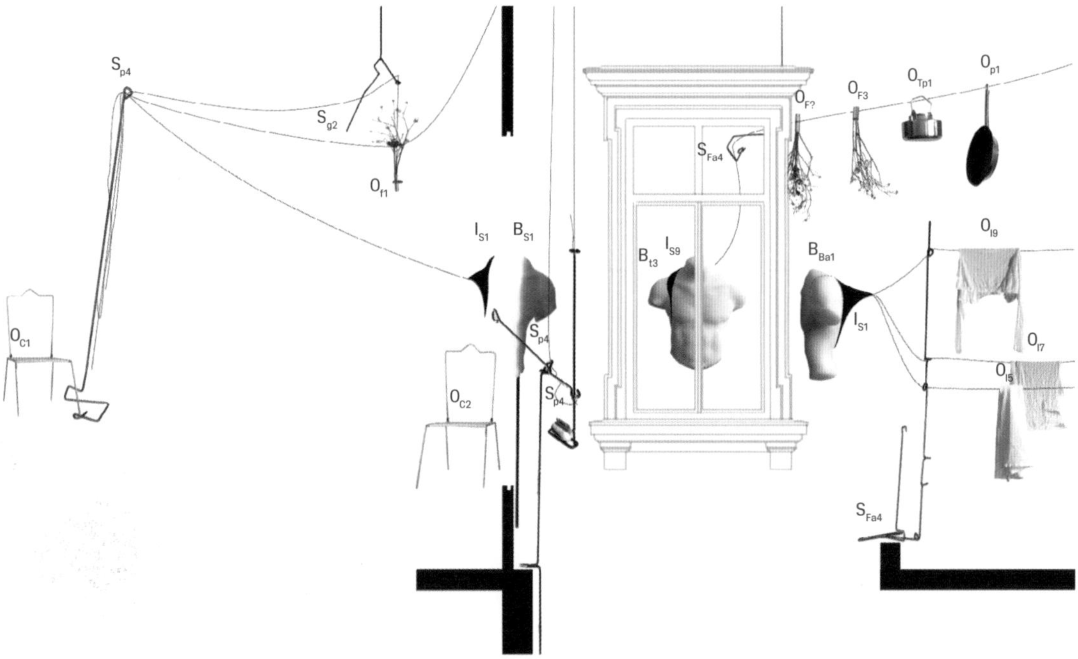

Bodies: Objects sequence section and notation

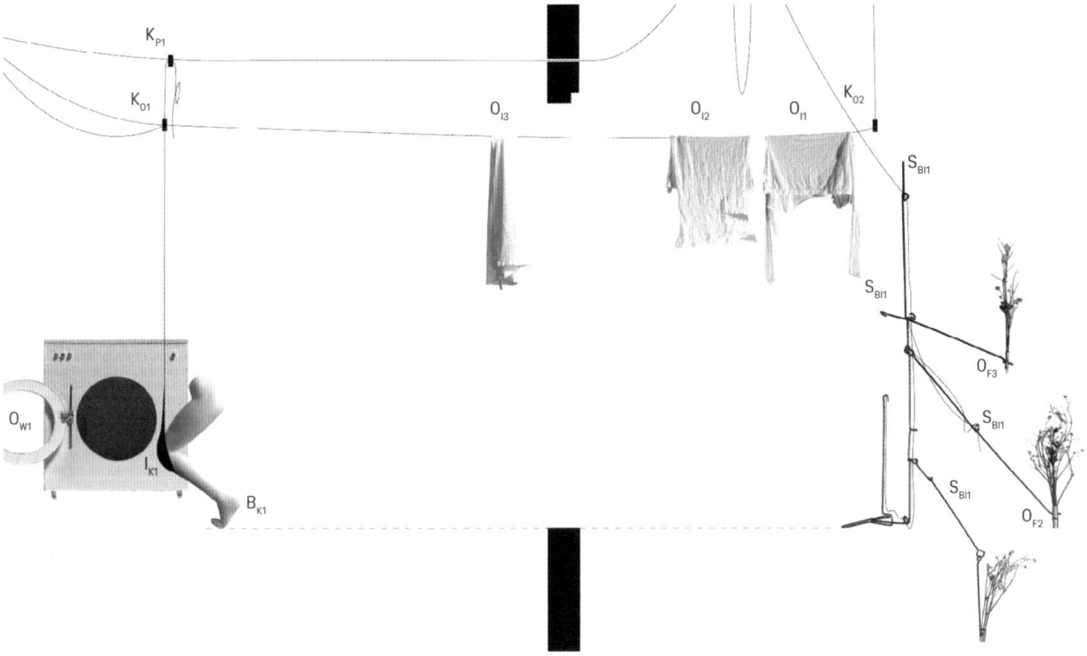

Laundry: Balcony sequence section and notation

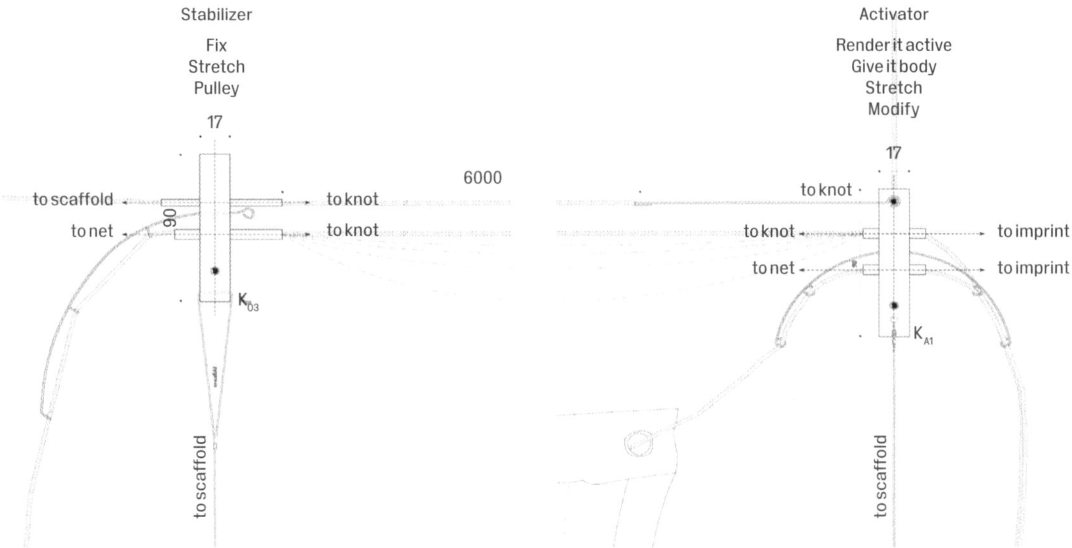

Structural knot sections

A view from a window out along the infinite cord world

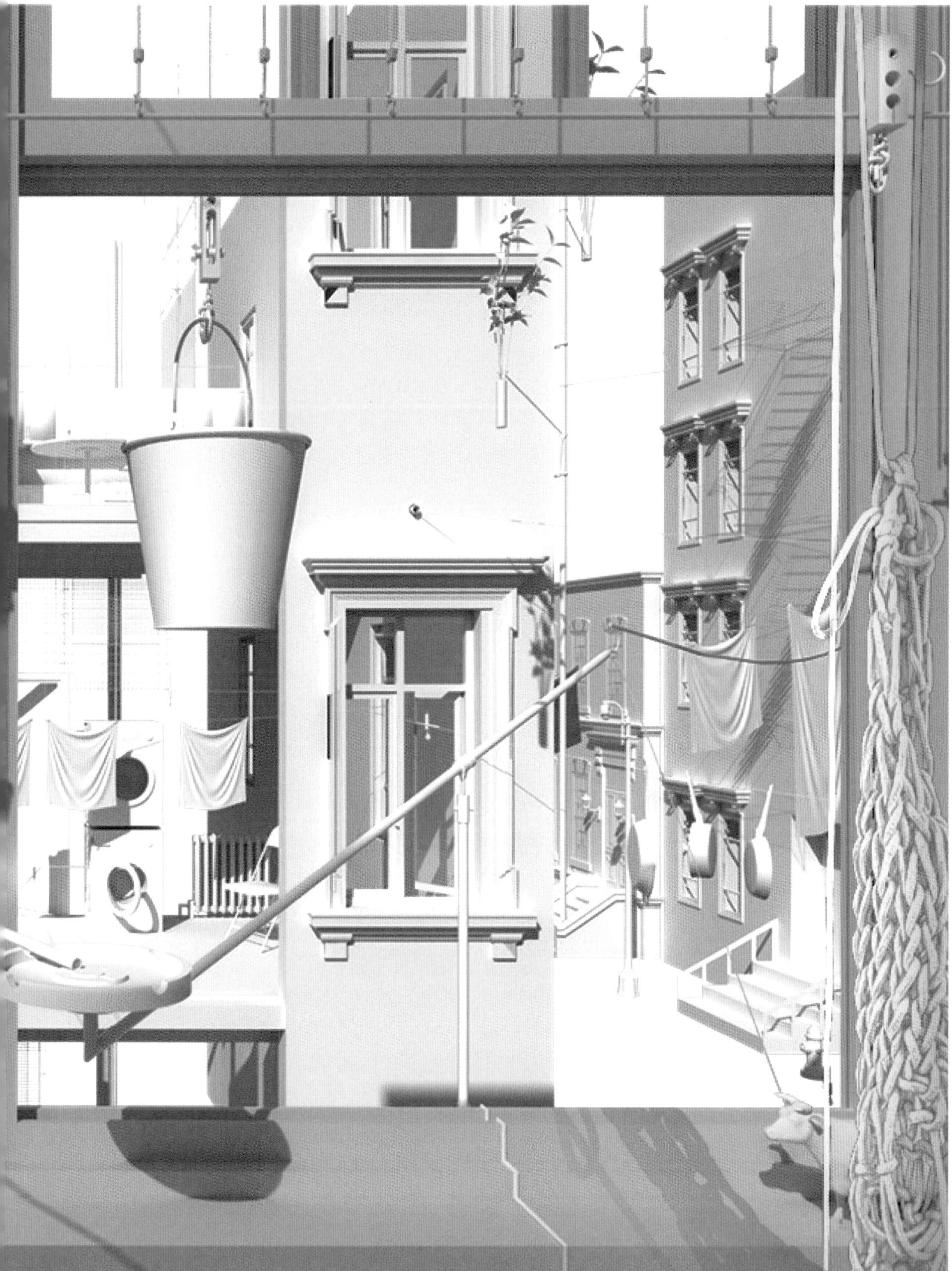

Hao Tang

The Knight's Loop

In the initial setup for the Chinese chess game, the pieces form an entanglement preventing a player from moving a checkmate-capable combination toward the opponent's king's box. To win, a player must somehow break down or punch holes into this fabric of chess pieces by creating pathways toward an arrangement capable of leading to checkmate. Chess pieces don't exist in isolation; they are associated with one another. When one piece moves it triggers the entire series of successive movements of the rest of them. As such, each chess piece is not a singular point but part of a powerful inertia with strong spatial fields.

So a woven piece informed by the game of chess should not be rigid or still. It should speak to a force that appears either on a smaller scale, such as within the weaving joints and connections, or a larger scale, like an architectural skin or structure. As if playing chess using wire, the project captures the dynamic movements of the pieces and transfers them into transformative structures. The current study ends on two scales, those of the body and the architectural skin.

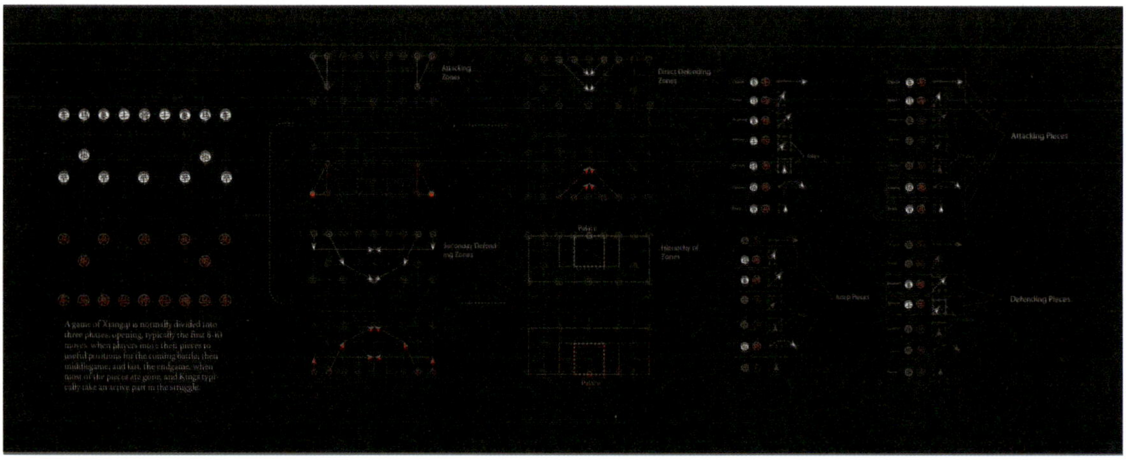

Chess movement diagram identifying the roles and hierarchy of chess pieces and the logic of their movements

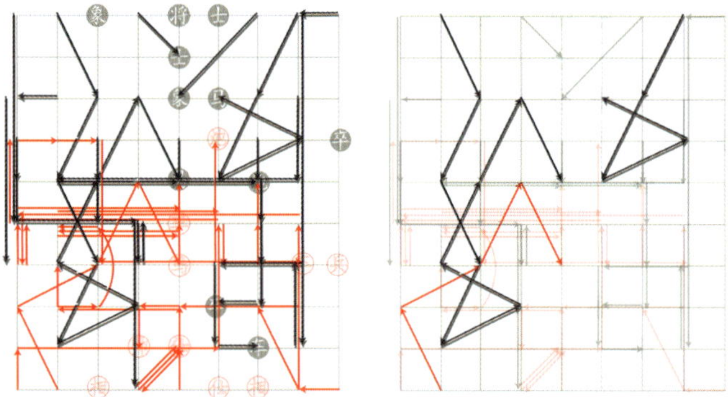

Drawings that trace a game of a famous chess player (left) revealing that knights tend to move circularly in a play (right)

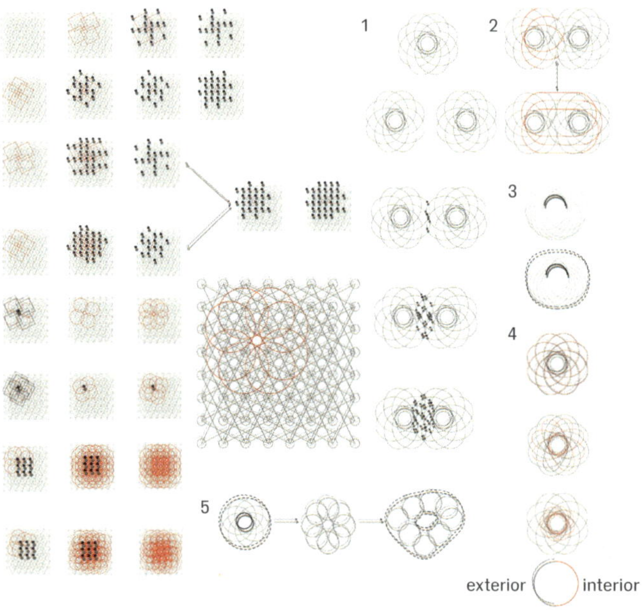

Diagram showing the structural patterns informed by knight movements on a chessboard and their possible weaving pattern

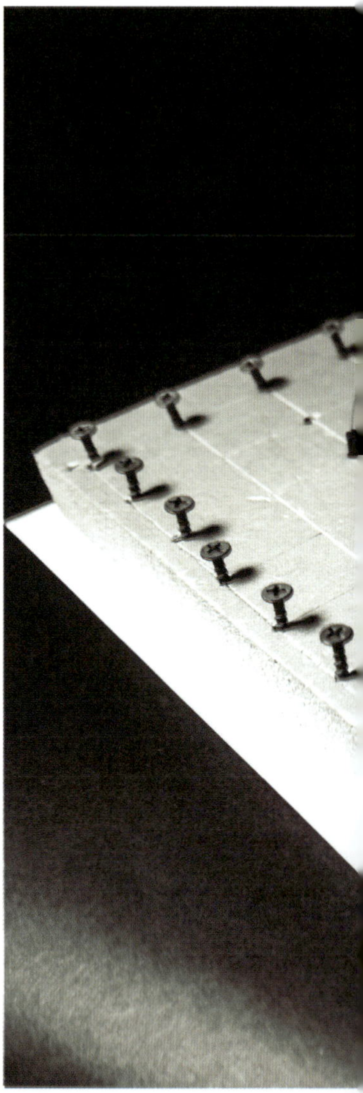

Study model of knight movements on an 8-by-8 grid board using wires

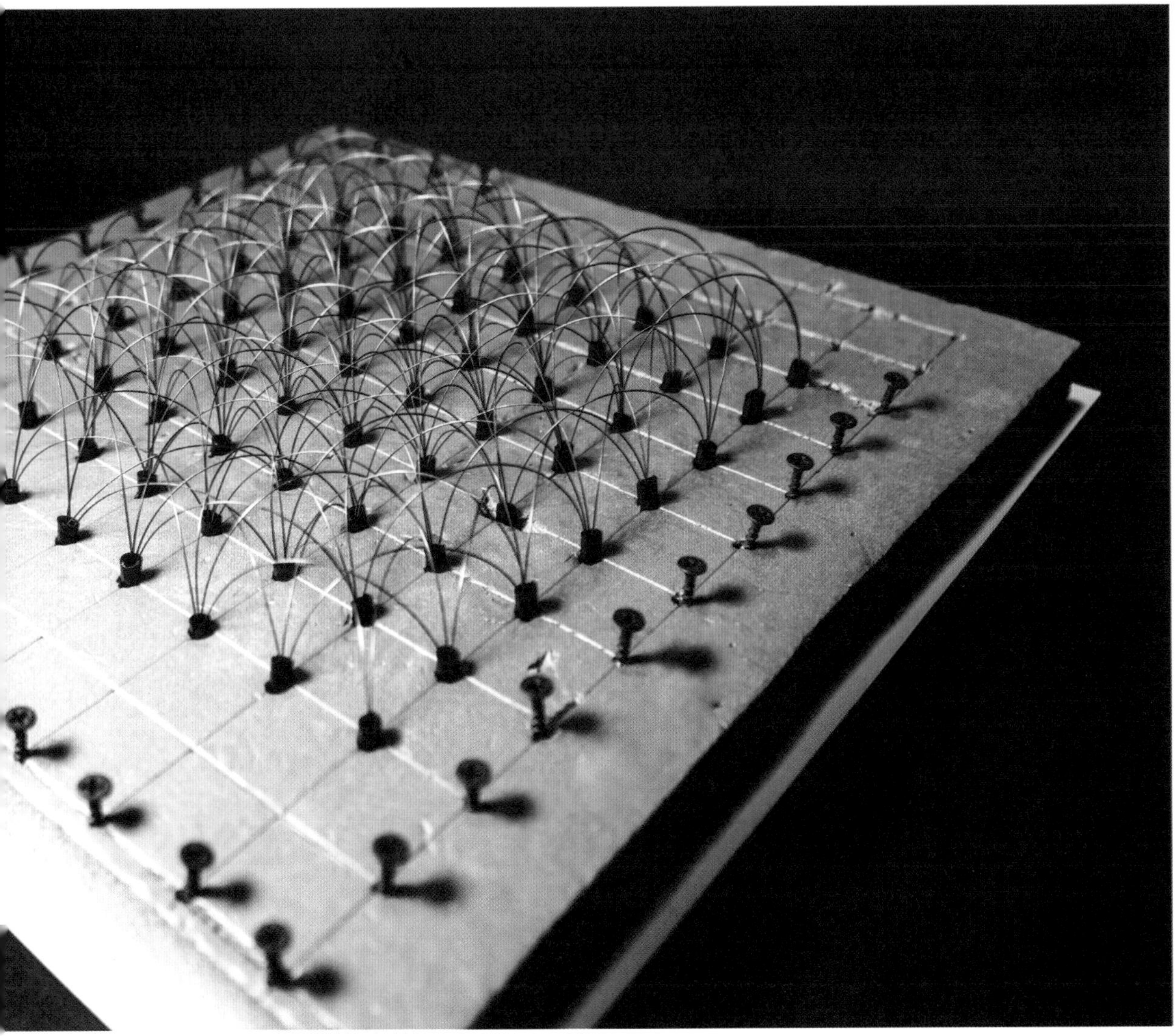

Study model of knight movements on an 8-by-8 grid board using wires

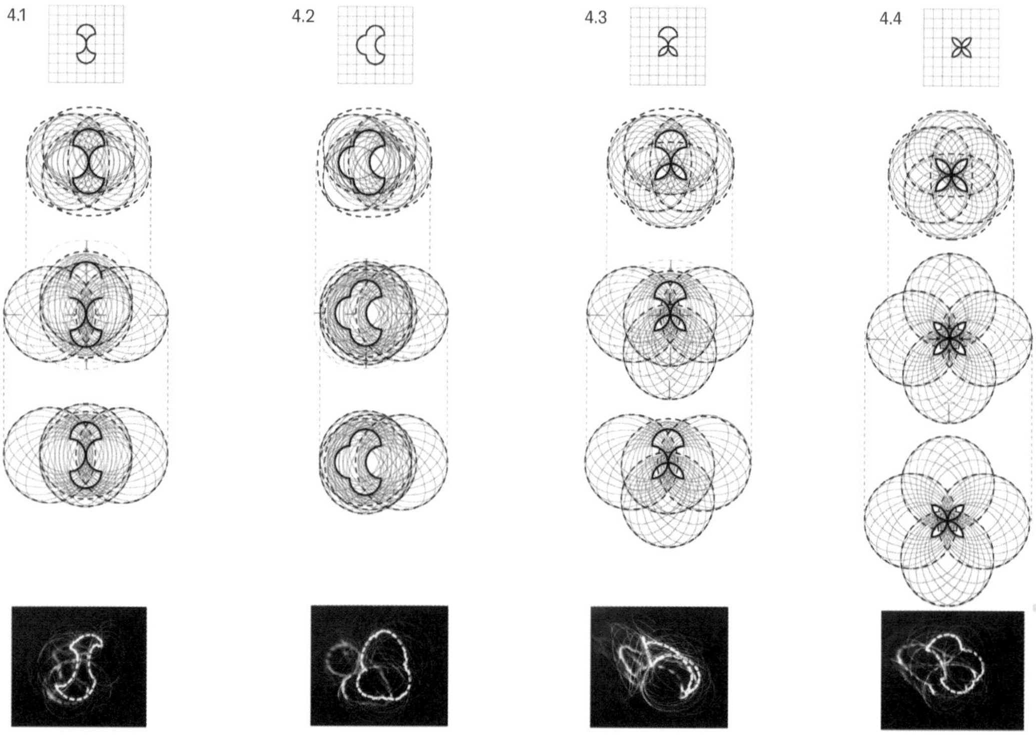

Complex weaving patterns and structures formed by knight's loops

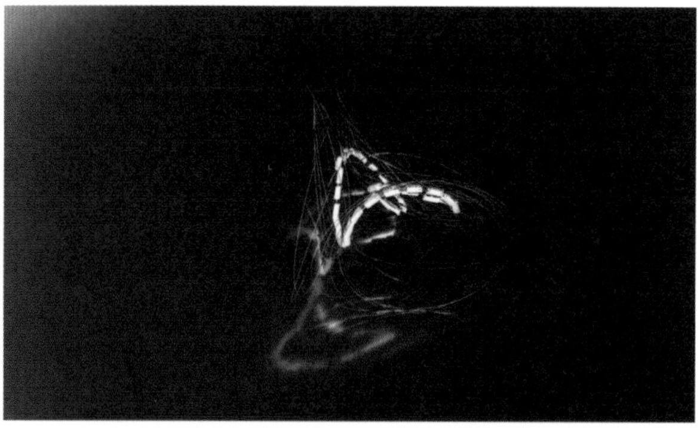

Model images: structural possibilities of the knight's movements in three-dimensional space

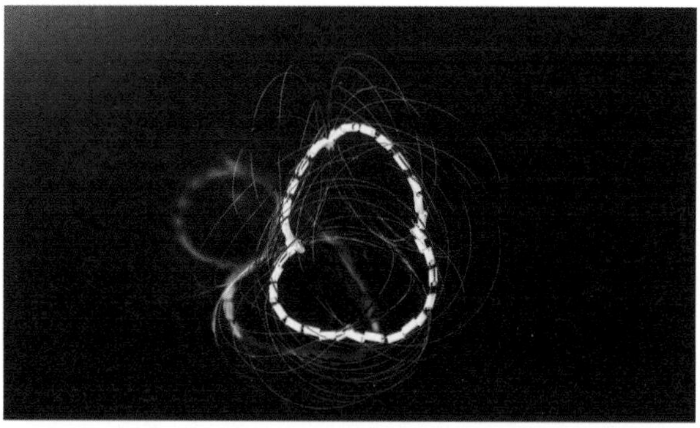

Model images: structural possibilities of the knight's movements in three-dimensional space

Model of complex structural pattern informed by knight movements (compressed structure)

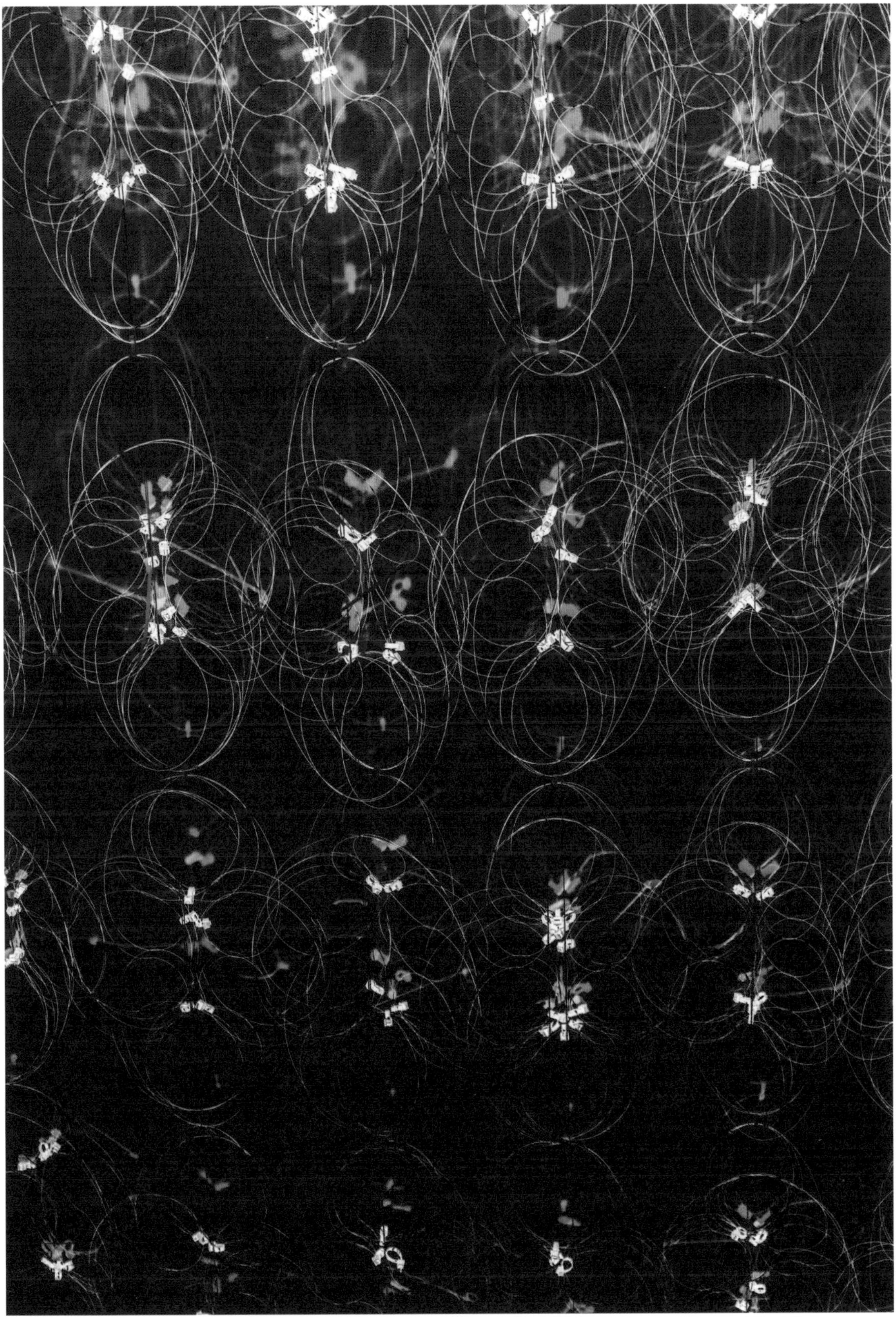

Model of complex structural pattern informed by knight movements (stretched structure)

Jun Nam

Bamboo Wife

This project undertakes a deconstruction of an Indigenous weaving technique as well as the meanings embodied in woven objects, followed by a reconstruction through contemporary discourse. Bamboo Wife, or Jook Bu-in, was a revered Indigenous pillow engineered to provide comfort through a simple form. A device that cools one's body during a summer day, it embodies both cultural heritage and individual intimacy, making it a mainstay in Korean culture for hundreds of years. Although it is an artifact born out of necessity, the name suggests it as an anthropomorphic symbol within social hierarchy referencing gender, age, and kinship, and its binary attachment, although diluted over time, is still intact.

The implications of the pillow permeate the social structure through its symbolic meanings, which have never been deconstructed to suit a contemporary world that demands blurring, crossing, and integrating. Its association with the Bamboo Wife is instinctual rather than intellectual or theoretical. Its tactile nature recalls the physical intimacy of one body with another, an increasingly uncommon communicative means.

Through processes of deconstructing and reconstructing that are based in handicrafts, the project aims to reorient the cultural meanings to contemporary society, where there is a dire need of engendering empathy among individuals, communities, and even objects. Through the haptic nature of the Indigenous weaving technique, the project envisions enabling tactile communication that promotes intimacy in the public realm.

Future inquiries that this project anticipates include the following: How can computation enter into Indigenous weaving? How can computational design maintain the integrity of traditional weaving? How can we rethink the role of architects within the revitalization of disappearing techniques, and what are the implications of the discourse itself?

Collage of movement

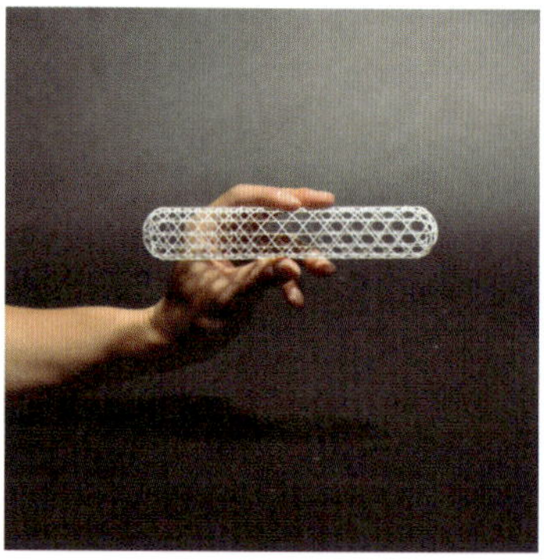

3D Printed Wife model

Instruction on How to make Bamboo Wife

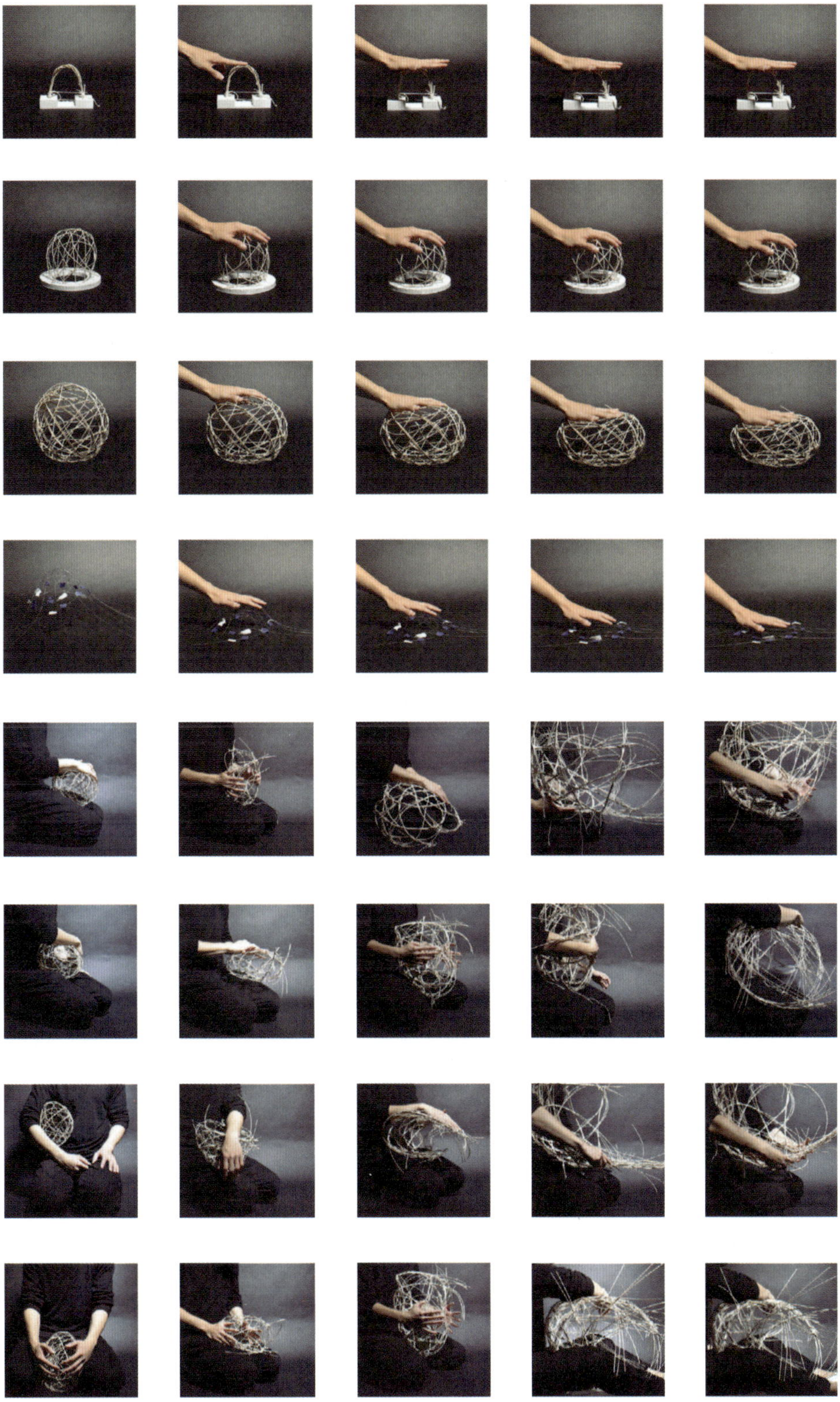

Demonstration of multiple mock-ups

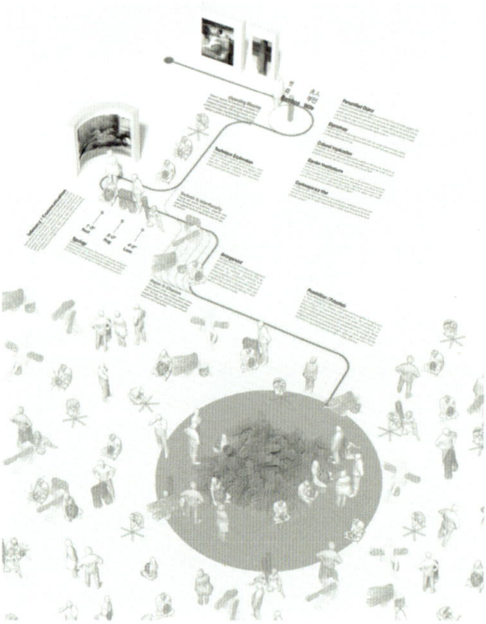

Process diagram

Hold Me

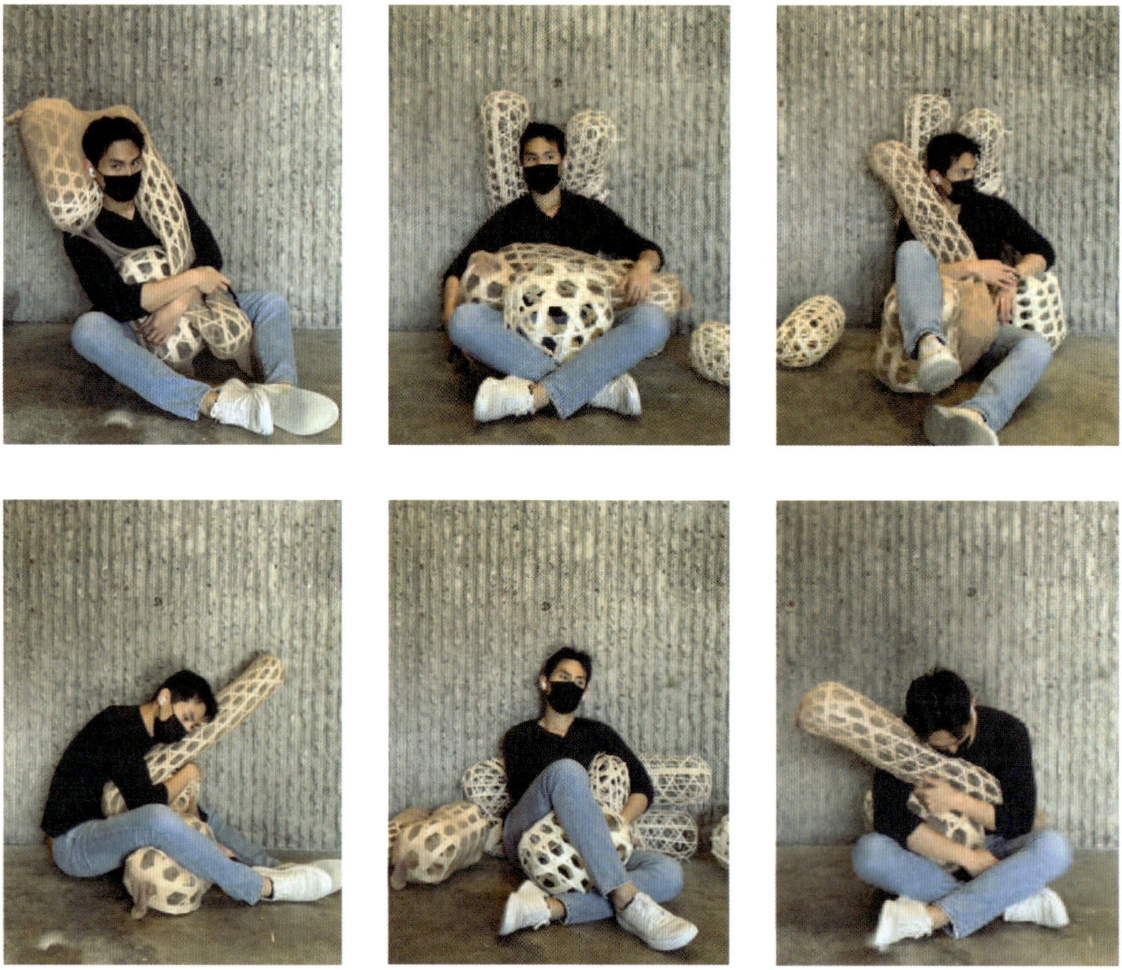

Prototype arrangement

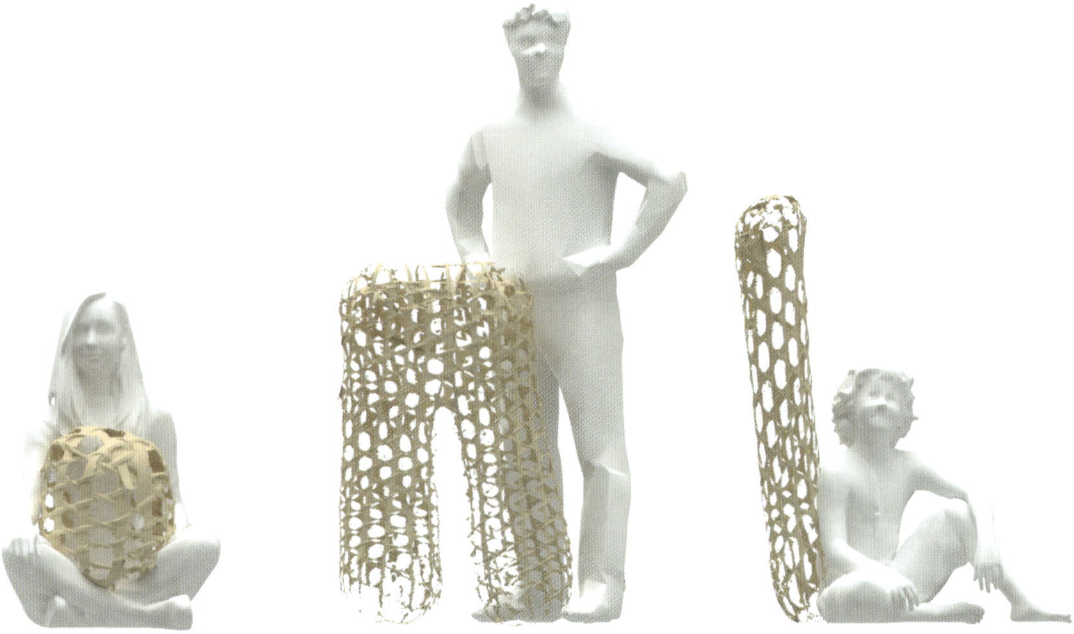

Typology diagram

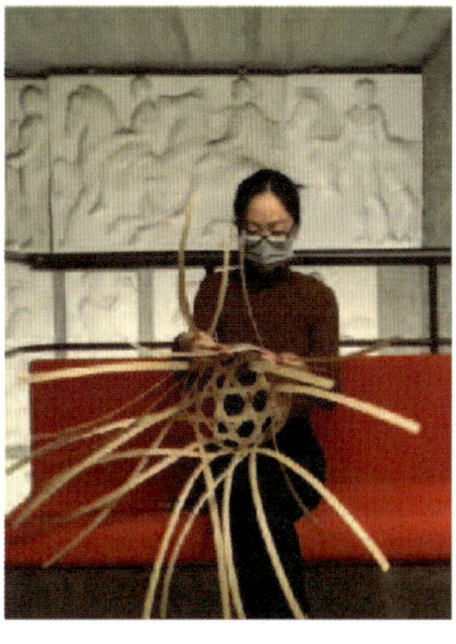

Prototype of shared methodology

Morgan Kerber

Woven

Weave Together: The Embodiment of Context within a Collectively Woven Textile

Woven is a space for conversation and collective making processes using innovative weaving techniques. Spanning 28 feet across, it is a canopy that defines a social and educational place for students to connect across undergraduate, graduate, PhD programs, and beyond. The design addresses the lack of means for encounters between students at school: having lost designated spaces for common activities and gathering, relationships are fostered interstitially and suddenly between desks and screens. The canopy embodies an ephemeral presence on an outdoor terrace to embrace collaborative activities that have been suspended in person due to the COVID-19 pandemic.

The basis of the weaving technique and inspiration for collective making are drawn from the textile traditions of the Haida Nation, the Indigenous population of the Haida Gwaii islands, off the coast of British Columbia, Canada. The Haida arrived to the archipelago even before large plant life, as evidenced by their oral histories and archaeological findings. The Daajing whaler's hat was the object chosen to exemplify Haida material culture. Its spruce-root weaving patterns represent a tale of place, familial relationships, function, and cultural memory.

The research initiated with an investigation into how form manifests through context, followed by an exploration of our own abilities to interpret context. There are two major force applications that can be applied to the woven fabric: spacing the strips evenly allows the fabric to shear and bend, while reorganizing the warps into bunches stiffens the fabric into a sheet—bundling, folding, stretching, bending, and separating. With these few actions hundreds of forms can be created, and the resilience and flexibility of the structure holds up over hundreds of rearrangements. One thing that became apparent during our research was that labor was highly valued in the Haida culture: The time spent creating these objects was used to communicate, and the labor of making was not just an application but also a material.

Woven together, made with reeds, red electrical tape and red Paracord

Woven together, made with reeds, red electrical tape and red Paracord

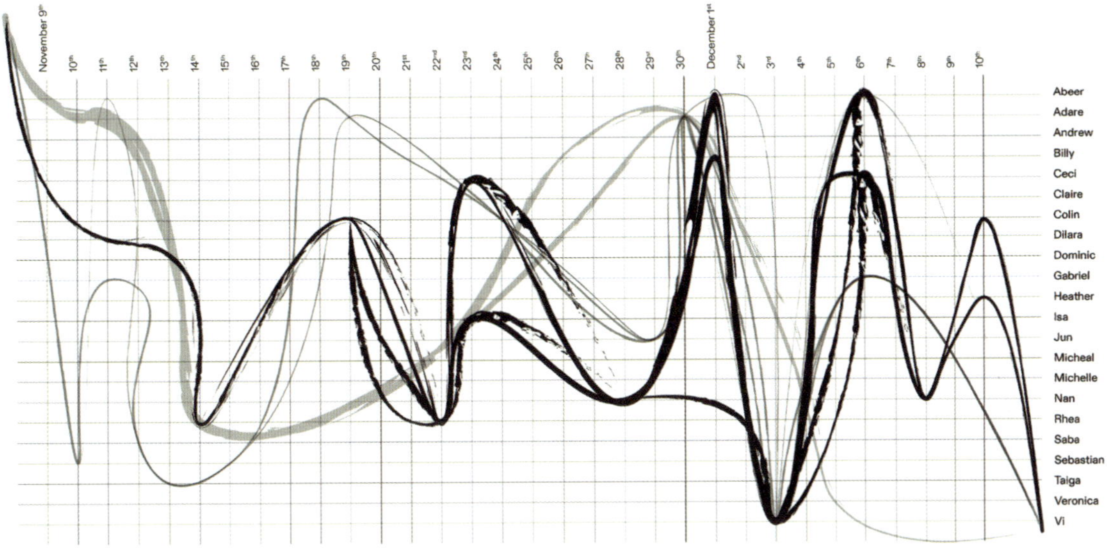

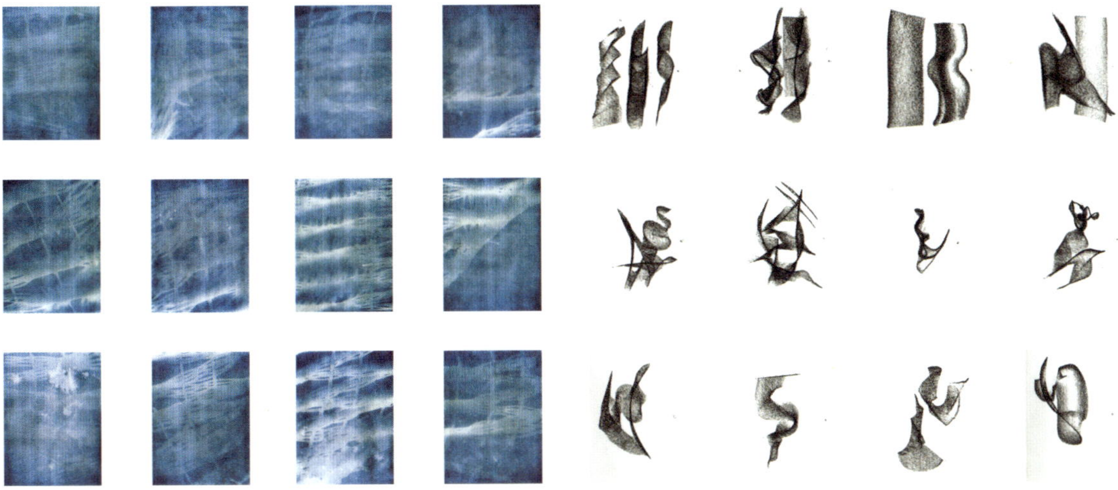

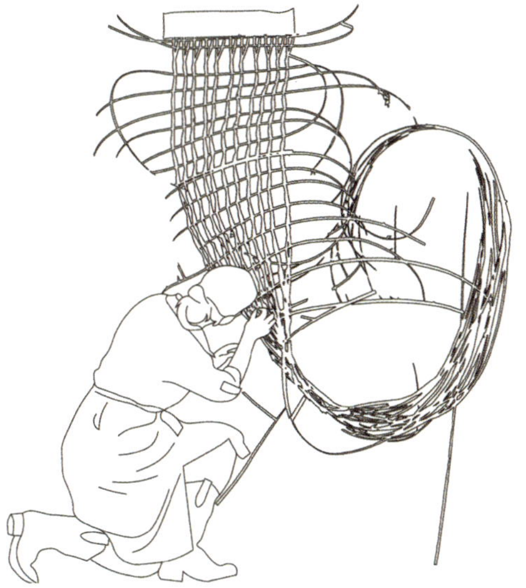

Collaborative process analysis

Sydney Maubert

Cartographies of Braiding

This project braids the land in a crude way using the bodies sunken beneath the collective memory of New Haven so that they rise to the surface. This was born out of two ideas: an article about bodies being unearthed and uprooted by fallen trees regularly from the New Haven Green which was also the end point of slavery in New Haven. The last person sold there was purchased for ten dollars and immediately emancipated. The project explores themes of value, femininity, and memory through braiding by giving women the authority to see and beautify themselves in familiar spaces. Braiding is an act women can simulate on their own or in the community, and as their ancestors are burrowed underground, they shore up into a kind of vaulted, braided architecture. The structures are close enough to the body to feel intimate yet expand far enough to gesture towards the public realm and communal nature of hair braiding. The braids are audacious like the women who make them, but they are functional, using a kind of catenary system by casing them in concrete hung upside down and flipping them over. These braidings become nomadic sites, deployed adjacent to the domestic realm next to the porch or in the backyard. Independently, they can generate a sense of domesticity in the urban realm and pay homage to the history in a public realm, like the Green. This object can be a generative thing where we can organically maintain our community, abstracted from languages and forms we understand. This proposes two iterations in New Haven: a public park and a memorial.

Render of braided vault, outdoor canopy

Hinge diagram of tubing technique

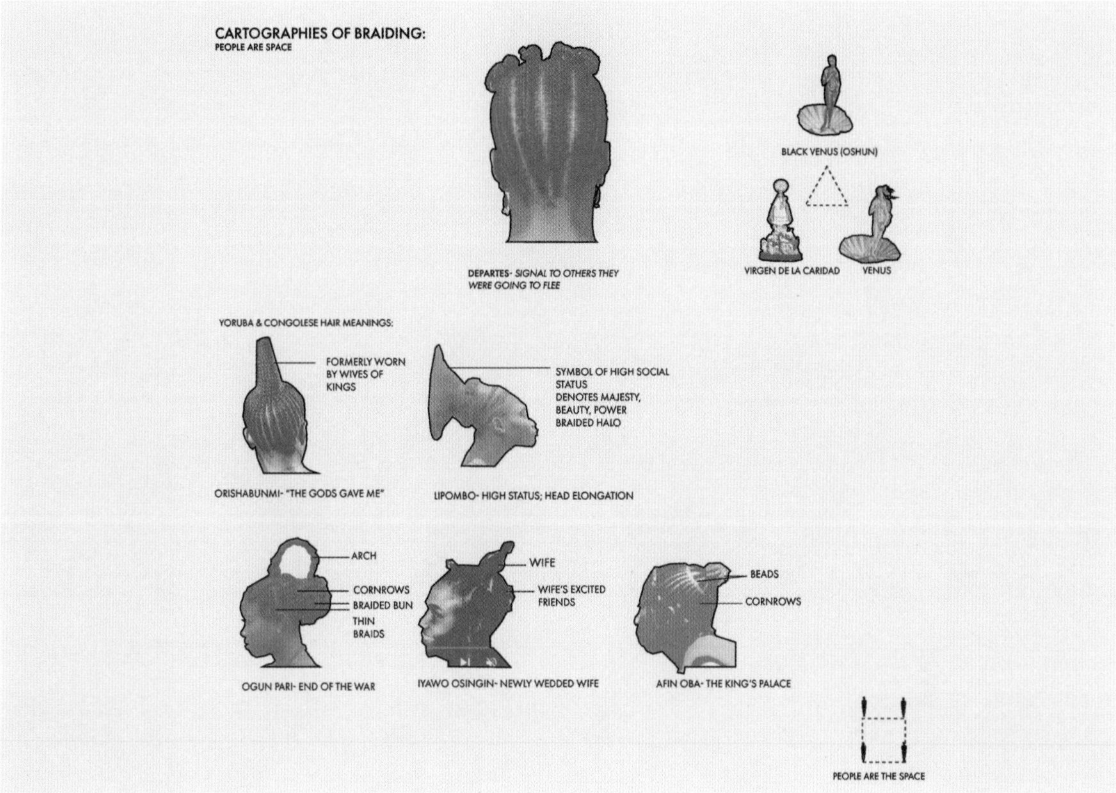

Yoruba hairstyles and their respective meanings, ranging from spiritual, status, or artistic. Collage and drawing

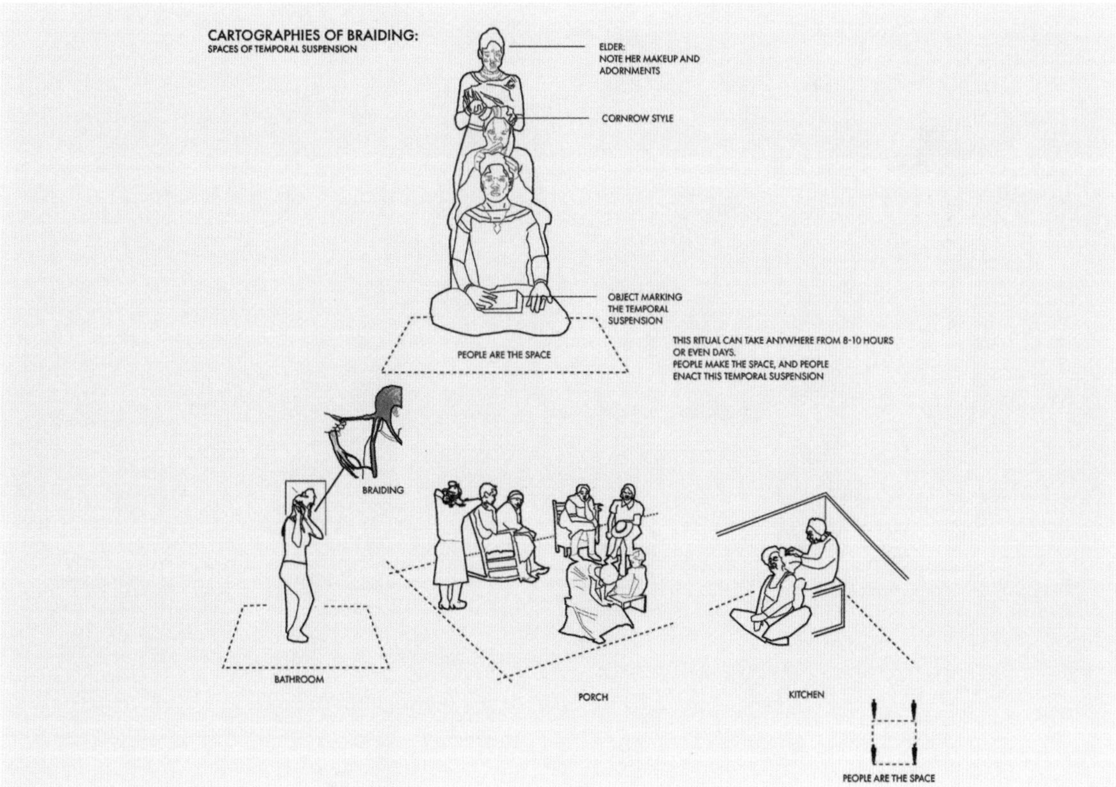

Drawing spatializing hair braiding, in the historical and contemporary sense

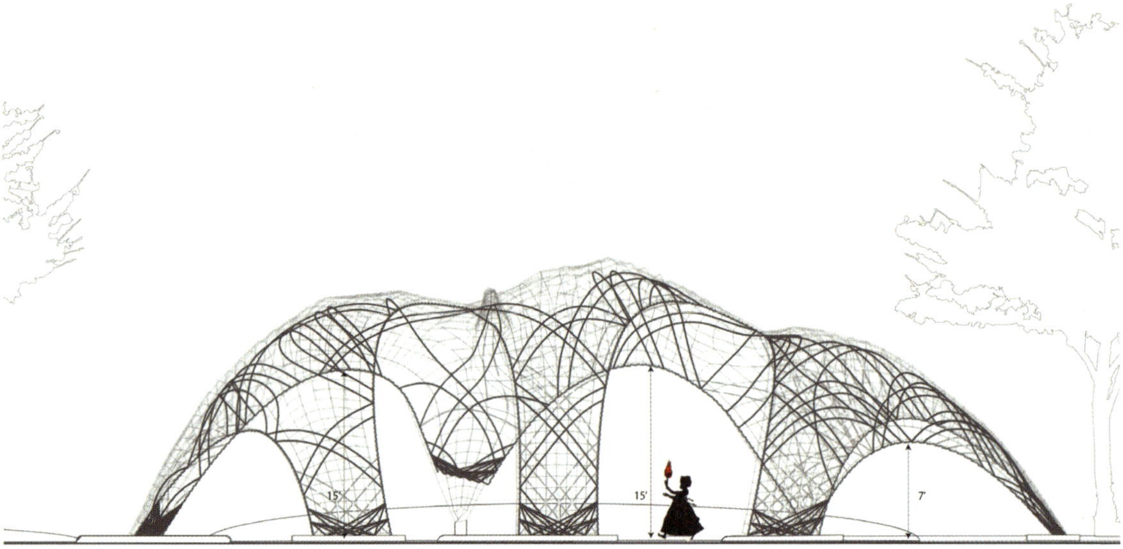

Proposed section drawing

Proposed axonometric site plan

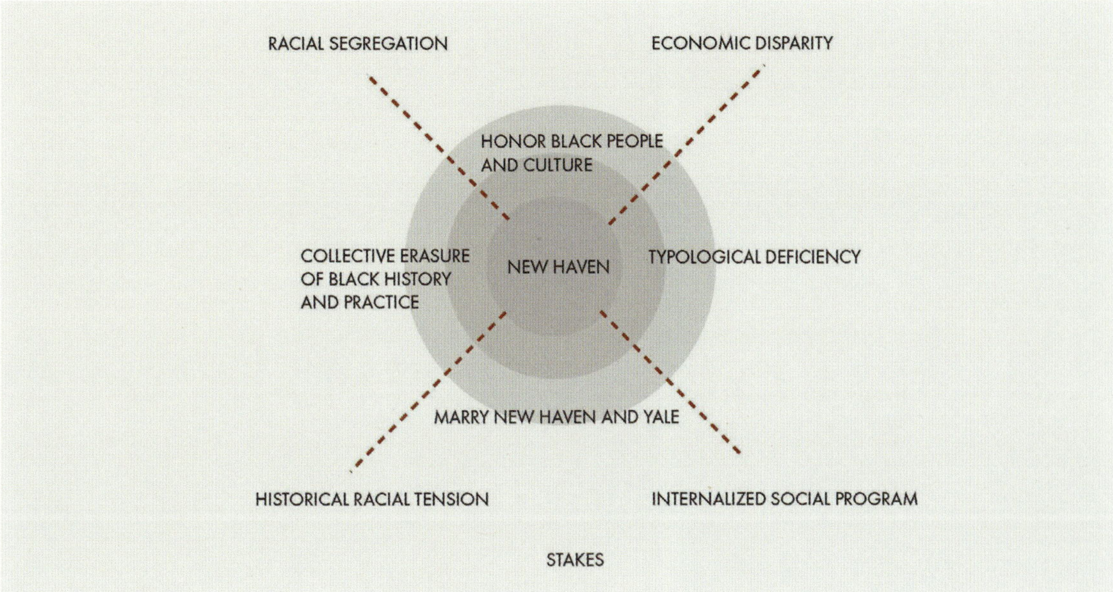

Diagram

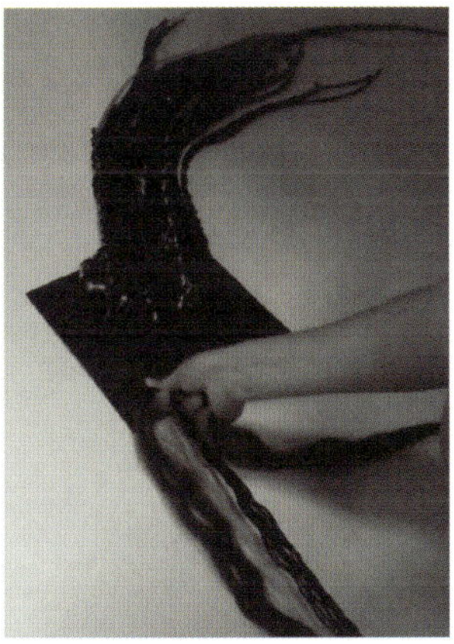

Fractal design research, visualizing hair braiding's history of mapping during transatlantic slavery, by simulating braiding itself on a cardboard sample.

Fractal design research, visualizing hair braiding's history of mapping during transatlantic slavery, by designing and braiding a wig out of yarn on a wig cap.

Quilt of New Haven.

Painted rendering proposal, mixed media tapestry

Smaranda Rusinaru

A Garment Tale

This project explores the notion of the hand as the "tool of all tools" and a way to infuse contemporary architecture with the "lived" quality of old handicrafts while contributing to better living situations and proper applications of new material constructions. The story of the Anthropocene Garment embodies conditions of making that are autonomous and spontaneous, collapsing back full circle. This process of creation began as an exploration of Indigenous crafts such as Navajo wedge weaving and then transforming them into systems of making with the potential to inform new processes of thinking architecture.

The Anthropocene Garment acts as a protective skin as well as a reflection of the burdens of the bodies that have carried the weight of nurturing and creating—and continue to be subjected to social and patriarchal domination. It is a blanket, an armor, and a metaphor. The beauty of the garment lies in its capacity to regenerate and grow. Designed through a continuous exploration of geometric patterns of rushing and adapted to respond to structural issues, the garment relaxes and contracts into pockets of various sizes that store, protect, and carry conceptual or mundane objects such as food, tools, infants, and ideas. The scale and context of the garment ranges from the Navajo world to mine and yours.

Navajo wedge weaving and processes of smocking, shirring, and folding

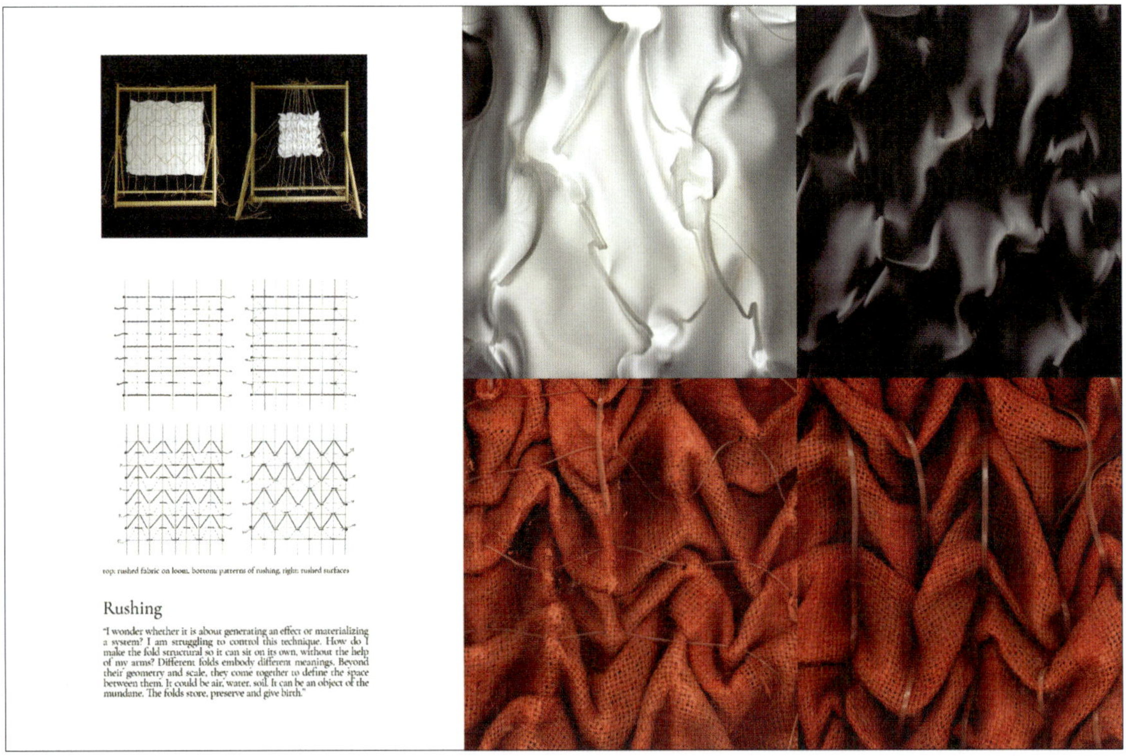

Processes of rushing

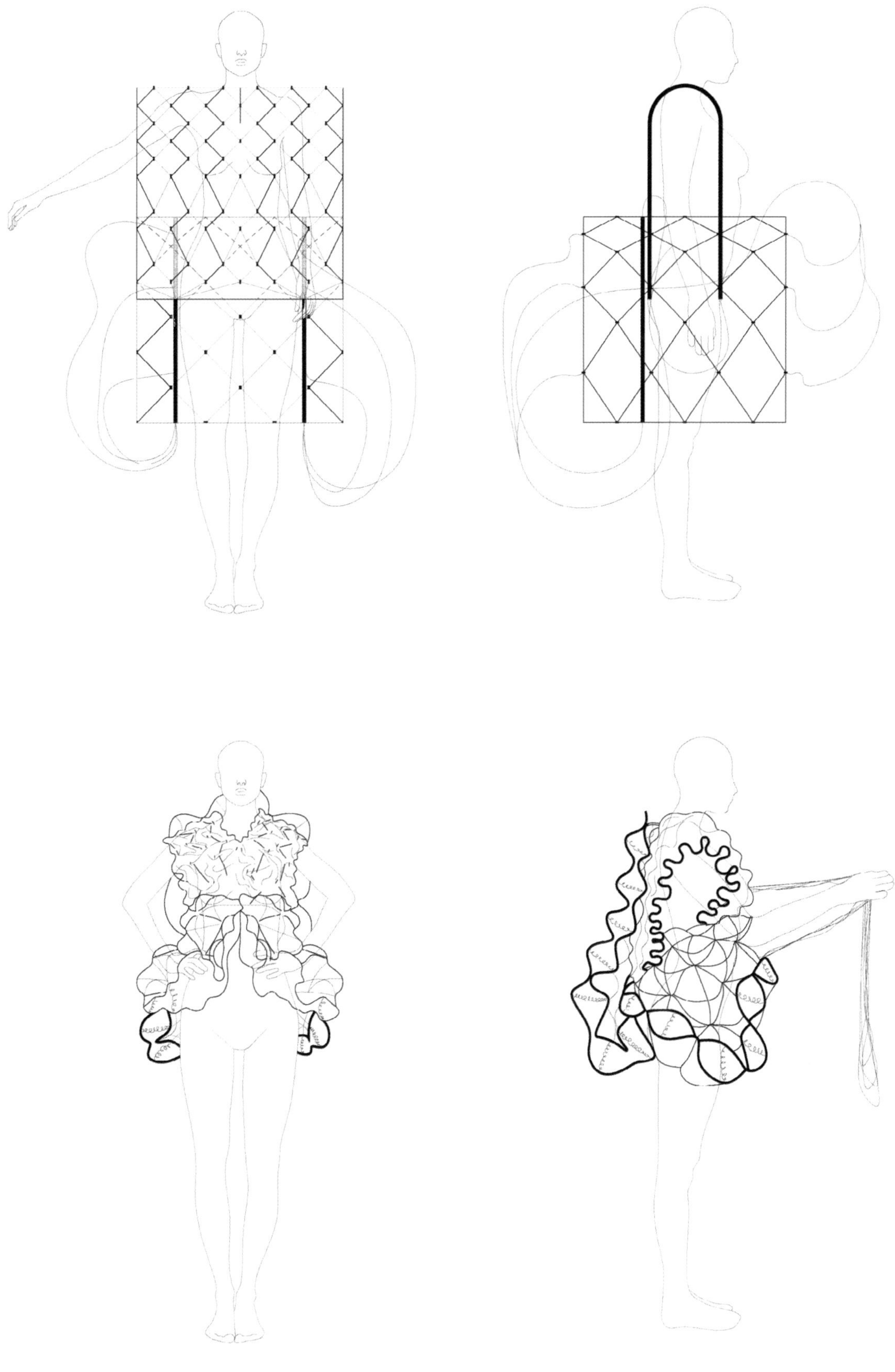

Elevations of the proposed garment both flat and rushed

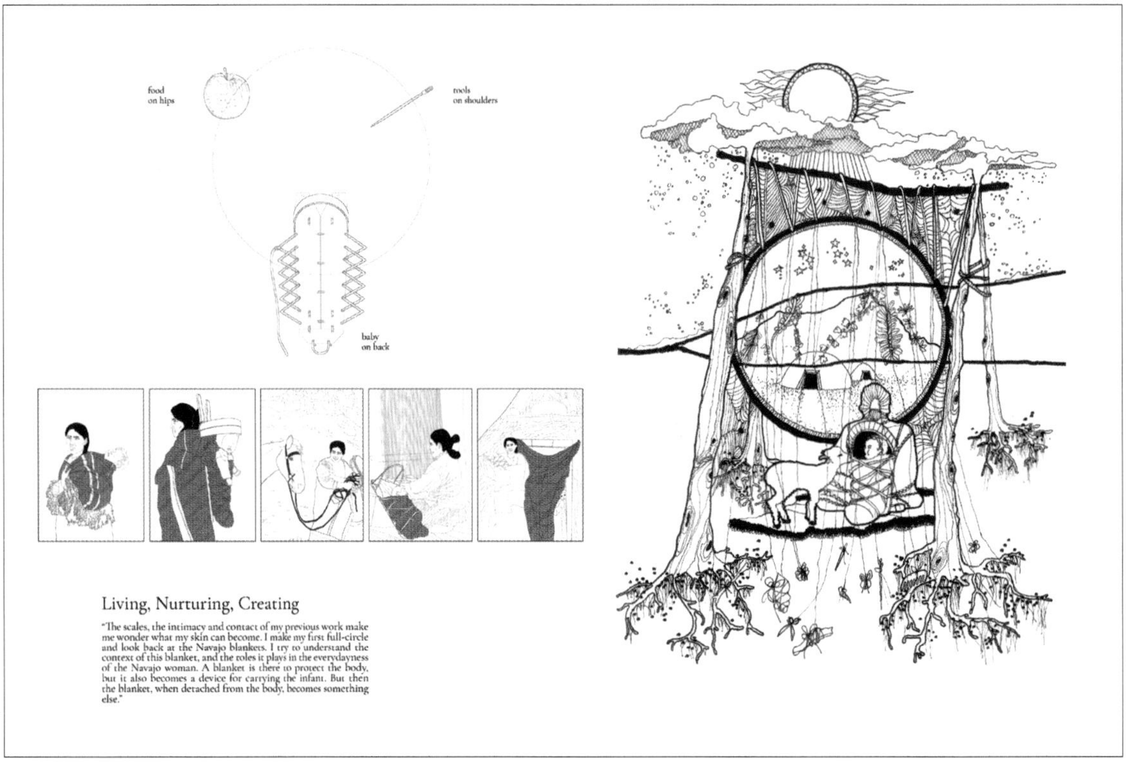

Application of the Navajo blanket

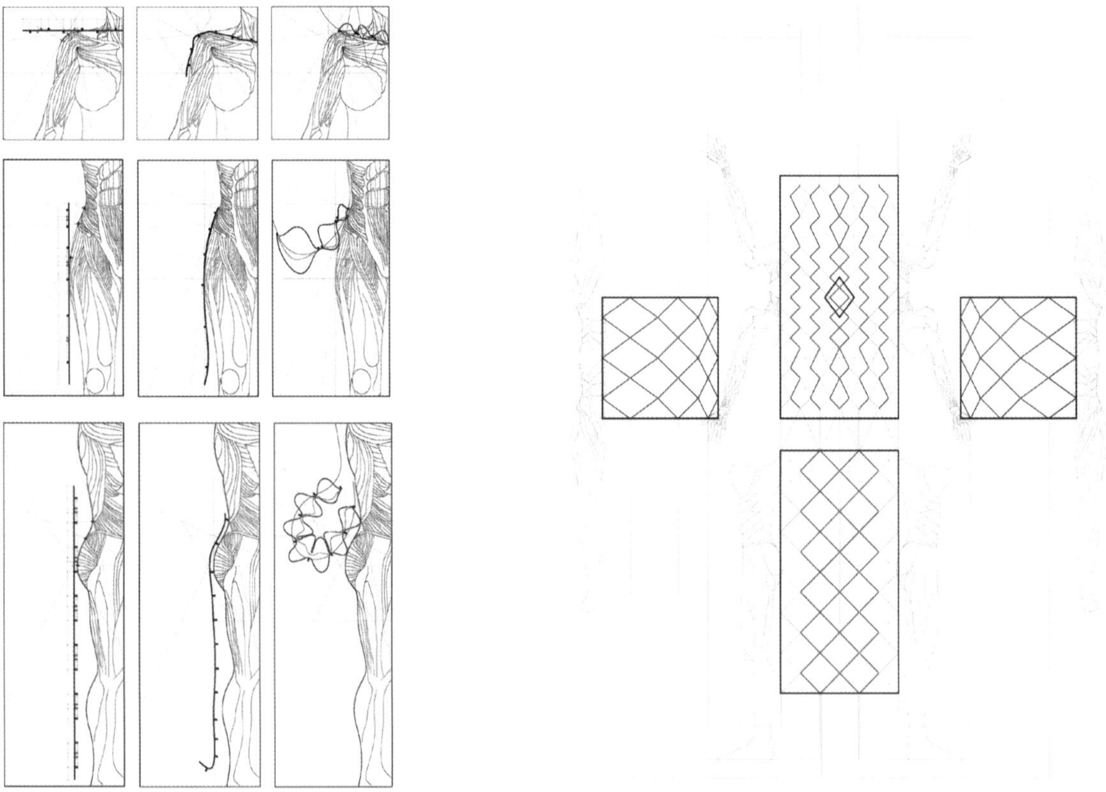

Sections and plan of proposed garment

May: *Picking*

July: *Resting*

October: *Gathering*

February: *Protecting*

Application of the proposed garment in different seasons and at different scales

1:1 Final garment in flat condition

1:1 Final garment carrying objects

Taiga Taba

In Flux

This project seeks the interstices between structure and fabric. They could be mutually exclusive but treated as analogous terms in various fields of inquiry. The Structural Fabric oscillates between the two conditions, blurring the distinction by creating a soft yet rigid architecture.

The process of making led to a reverse-engineering strategy in pursuit of a particular effect exploiting a selected technique rather than a context-driven strategy. After the effect was attained through numerous exercises, I searched for a specific site where it could be applied.

As a place confronted with frequent earthquakes, Japan seemed a suitable site for intervention, since the competence of its structures is under constant scrutiny. My Structural Fabric serves as a second layer for structurally unsound buildings, draped over the exterior to support the building externally. Through operations like binding and locking, the fabric becomes structural yet easy to disassemble and apply elsewhere.

Applying structural fabric to dilapidated apartments on Kiyosuna Street in Tokyo (1927–2002)

Physical model (1:50)

Physical model (1:50)

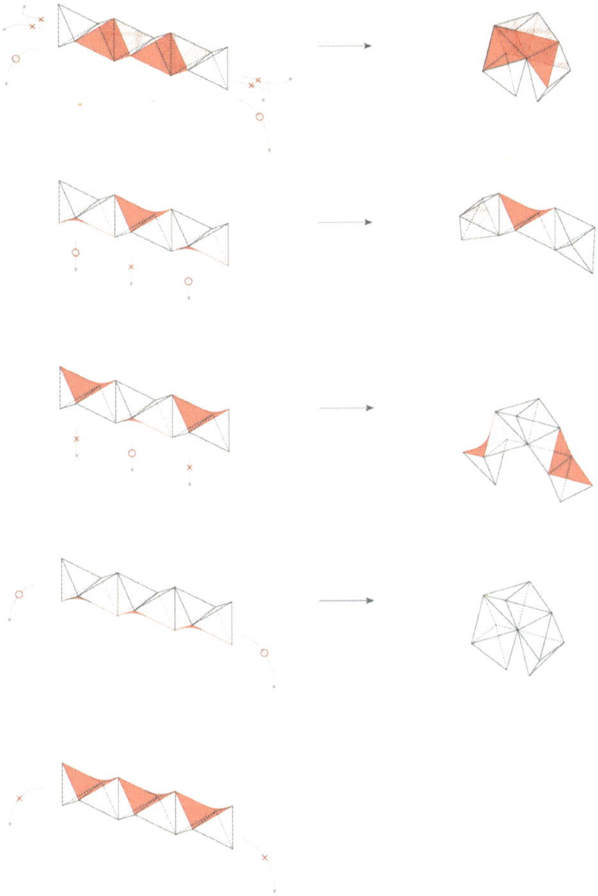

Behavioral diagram of tubing technique

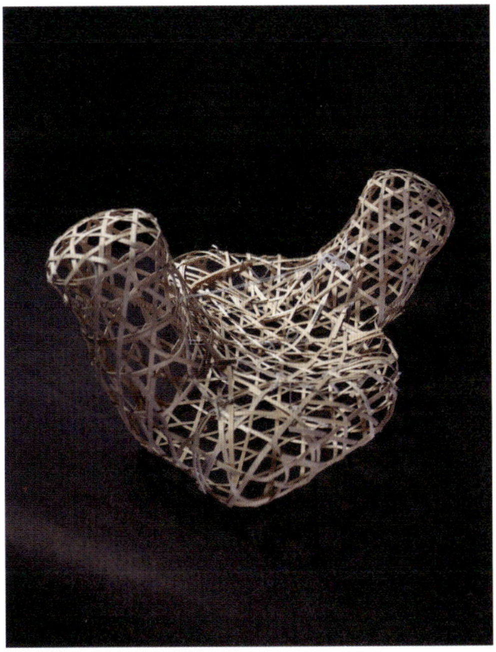

Process model of technique 1: bamboo weaving

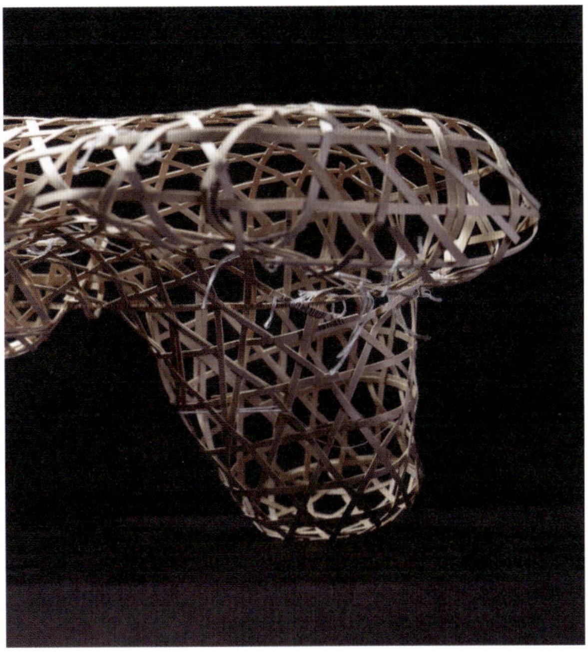

Process model of technique 1: bamboo weaving

Process model of technique 2: tubing

Process model of technique 3: beading

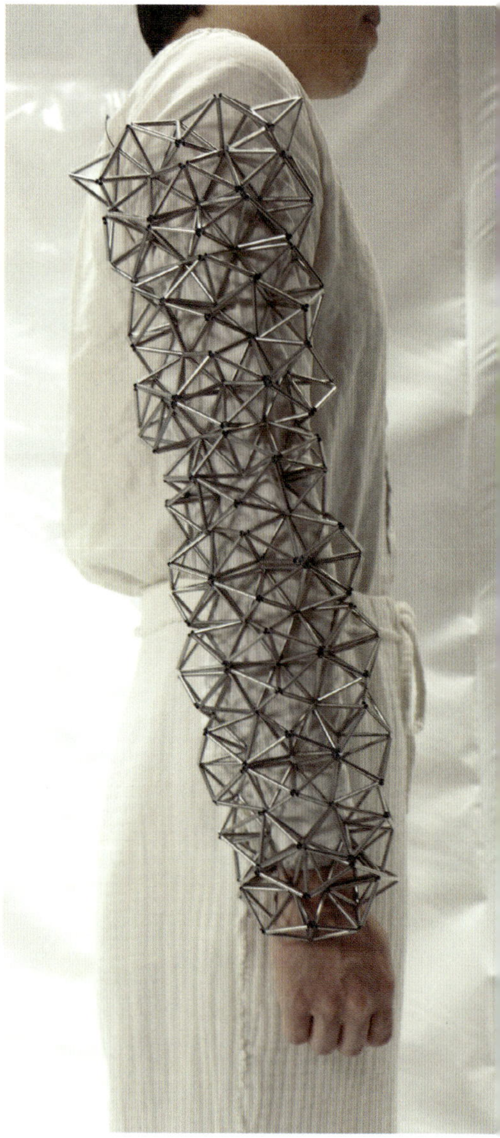

Demonstration of structural fabric

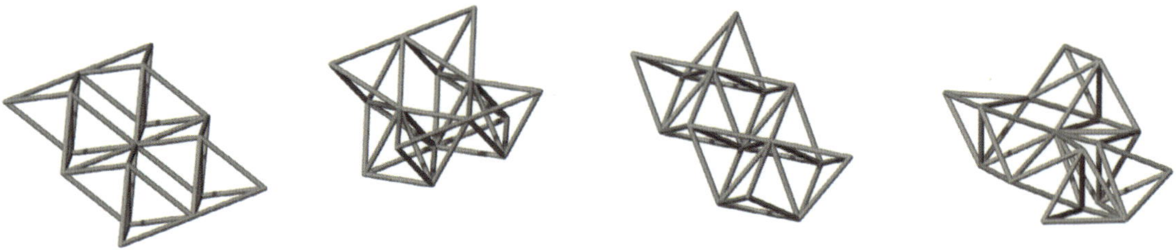

Hinge diagram of tubing technique

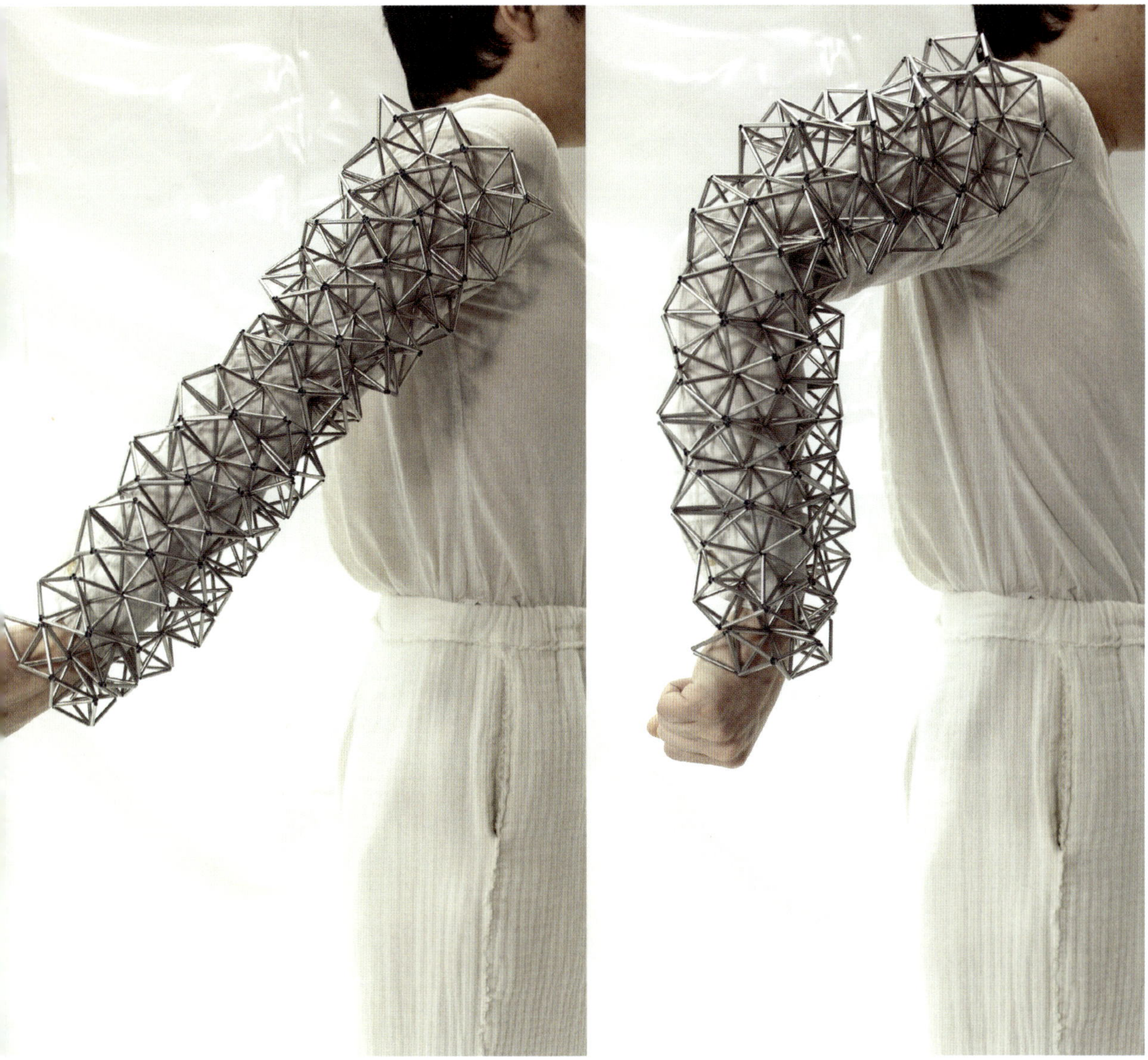

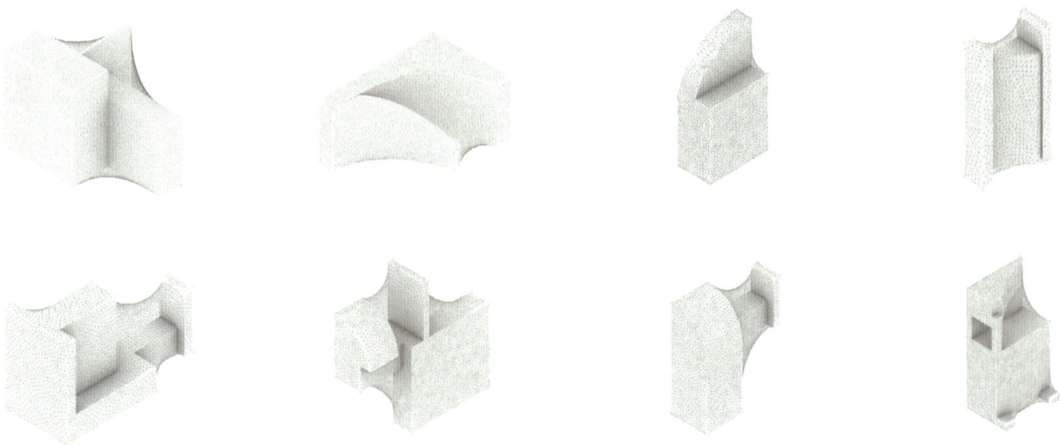

Shrink-wrap simulation as an elaboration of drapery

IMAGE CREDITS

Nick Zukausakas
14

Timothy Hursley
17

Domicile Thunder Moon
19

Tom Harris
21

Rodney Leon Architect
68, 72

John Bartelstone Photography
74

Abeer Seikaly
146, 159, 160, 163

Paul Tahon
150

Dreamclay
163 top

Stav Dror
163 bottom, 164, top and bottom, 167